J. B. Bury, E.A. Barber, Edwyn Bevan...

The History of Hellenistic Period

OK Publishing 2021

J. B. Bury, E.A. Barber, Edwyn Bevan…
The History of Hellenistic Period

Published by
MUSAICUM
Books

- Advanced Digital Solutions & High-Quality book Formatting -

musaicumbooks@okpublishing.info

2021 OK Publishing

ISBN 978-80-272-7292-1

Authors

J. B. Bury
E.A. Barber
Edwyn Bevan
W.W. Tarn

Contents

The Hellenistic Age and the History of Civilization

THE habit of treating what is, not very happily, called the Hellenistic age as if it were no more than a wayside inn in which a historical student travelling from Athens and Sparta to Rome is forced reluctantly to halt for a few tedious hours is not yet obsolete. This short survey is designed to illustrate and underline its importance and interest for the subsequent history of civilization.

The period of Greek history from the conquest of Alexander the Great, who worked a miracle that seemed to break the continuous course of history by a long leap, down to Rome's completion of her Eastern conquests by the annexation of Egypt, has been until comparatively recent years exceptionally unfortunate, in not being studied for its own sake, and therefore in not having its definite and eminent place in the general history of the world properly understood. It has entered little into liberal education except so far as it is involved in the history of the Roman Republic. An ordinary reader of Roman history will just hear of the brilliant Academician Carneades and the wise Stoic Panaetius of Rhodes, because they visited and impressed Rome; but he knows hardly anything as a rule of the Greece in which these men of light and leading had been brought up. The art of that period can not be ignored; it appeals to the eye, in originals or copies, in every large European collection; but the visitor to the museums who knows all about the ages of Pheidias and Praxiteles is astonishingly ignorant of the world in which the Venus of Melos or the Dying Gaul was chiselled. A generation ago boys used to learn geometry in the handbook of Euclid, but the few who had a vague notion that "Euclid" was the name of the author had no idea who he was or when he lived; if he had lived in the fifth century and not in the age of Ptolemy Soter, many of the schoolboys, and possibly some of the masters, would have known at least that he was a Greek. For there was a notion prevalent that the Greeks were already decadent in the third century; it has perhaps hardly died out yet, and has probably been the principal cause of the neglect of the post-Demosthenic age. Nothing could be more untrue. That vague and facile word "decadent" is often misused, but no misuse could be more flagrant than to apply it to the Greeks of the third and second centuries. The age of the political greatness of their cities was indeed over, but they still possessed creative strength and were as hot as ever on the quest of truth. In completely altered circumstances they were doing new and valuable things and were expressing the Hellenic spirit in new and valuable ways. Their highest intellectual endeavours were now in the field of the exact sciences and this was the age of their greatest mathematicians.

For anyone who is interested in exploring the history of European civilization and finding out how the past is stored in the present, this period of Hellenism may be said in a certain way to count more than the age of the independent city states ; for it was through this period that the earlier age exerted its influence. It was in this period that the culture of Rome was semi-hellenized and it was through Rome that Greece leavened the civilization of Western Europe. We must remember that when a Roman went to Athens or Rhodes or Alexandria he imbibed the ideas a11d culture of the living Greece of the time ; this training would include a knowledge of her past, but the past would be seen by him as by a native Greek through the glasses of the present. The Latin poets (except Horace) in t;he first century B. c. owed more to the comparatively modern Greek poets, the Alexandrines, than they owed to the older and greater poets of the great age of Hellas; and it was the contemporary art of Greece that appealed to the taste of Roman connoisseurs and supplied models to Roman artists.

To judge the value of any section in the line of human events for the progress of civilization and to apprehend its significance for the sections that followed, it is not enough to make a catalogue of the achievements at1d the discoveries. We cannot appreciate it by bare outstanding results. We must recreate the life of the age for its own sake,seek to live it over again and to understand the problems which faced the rulers and the thinkers and how they tried to solve them.

To aid us in making the attempt, we have now much more material than Droysen had, when he wrote his valuable *History of Hellenism*. Within the last generation the discovery of a mass of con temporary documents, inscriptions, and still more papyri, has given a powerful stimulus to the study of the period, and for a good many years past a number of savants have been engaged on an intensive study of the political, economic, and social life under the Macedonian monarchies. But the results of their work have so far hardly penetrated beyond learned circles into the general knowledge of the educated public.

The period is itself extraordinarily interesting, though it is a period in which there is no difficulty in losing one's way. The change so suddenly wrought by Alexander in his ten mirac- ulous years, substituting European for Asiatic rule all over the Near East, set problems which no European statesman had ever had to face before. The new rulers had to steer their ships over unfamiliar waters by strange stars. Large political and social problems were raised. New material and unexpected opportunities were given to Greek science, to advance in its endeavors to comprehend man's environment. The change meant an economic revolution resembling, on a smaller scale, that which was brought about by the discovery of the lands of the Western hemisphere and the circumnavigation of the earth eighteen hundred years later.

The effect of this revolution was that between the fourth century and the end of the third a long step was taken on the road which separates our civilization to-day from that of the fifth century B.C. That is another way of putting Mr Tarn's observation about the third century that it strikes one as comparatively "modern." If a European of today were precipitated backward through time by a sorcerer's spell into some Hellenic town of the past he would much sooner get used to his new surroundings, if they were in one of the great Greek cities founded by the Macedonians, Alexandria or Seleucia or Antioch, than if he were cast into the Athens or Syracuse of a hundred years further back. There was business enterprise on a considerable scale. The seas were not deserted by ships in winter, as they had been in the previous century. Now that Eastern trade had been thrown open to Greeks, the profits to be made were so large that merchants braved the dangers of winter voyages in a way that in old days was unknown. It has been suggested that the popular astronomical poem of Aratus which was so much admired by the ancients was composed with a11 eye to the need of a handbook for mariners. It is on the practical uses of astronomical knowledge that the poet insists. The volume of trade had grown so large that banking a11d exchange assumed great importance. The monetary transactions of this period, the state banks of Egypt, the international bank of Rhodes, were as far beyond the vision of the Delphic priests, or of Pasion and his clients in the days of Demosthenes, as the banking business of modern times was beyond the vision of the founders of the Bank of England.

The society of this age was tolerant; people did not trouble much about the beliefs of their neighbours; thought was perfectly free. The power of the Olympian gods, who had now to share their divinity with mortal potentates, was virtually over. There was only one deity in whom nearly every one believed, the goddess Fortune. If people did not know that the earth moves, it was now part of common knowledge that the earth is round; and the gibes with which Aristophanes derided Socrates for trying to compute its diameter or circumference would now have fallen flat.

There had indeed been one occasion when the existence of the philosophical schools of Athens was seriously threatened, not however for orthodox but for political reasons, a11d the episode is of consider able interest. It happened when the democracy was restored on the ar- rival of King Demetrius in B.c.307, and Demetrius of Phalerum, head of the government which was overthrown, had to flee. New laws were drawn up and one of these, proposed by a certain Sophocles of Sunium, suppressed the philosophical schools,the Academe and the Peripatos,and ordained that no such school should be established in future without the licence of the state. The law was aimed particularly at the Peripatetics because the head of that school, Theophrastus, had been an intimate friend and adviser of Demetrius of Phalerum. The law was passed and Theophrastus left Athens, but public opinion changed in a few weeks or months. The Atheni- ans felt that Socrates and Plato and Aristotle could not be described as friends of democracy, yet their genius had largely contributed to building up the reputation of the city as the centre of Hellenic culture. As a matter of fact it was discovered that the law was illegal. The legal position of the schools was that of religious clubs devoted to the worship of the Muses, and religious clubs had been recognized as legal institutions by a law of Solon. Accordingly a *graphe paranomon* lay against Stratocles; it was brought by a pupil of Theophrastus,and Stratocles lost his case,although he was defended by Demochares from whose mouth, in attacking Socrates and Plato and Aristotle and other less famous philosophers, such pearls of abuse rained as Greek orators were adepts in producing when they were in a vituperative mood. If such a law had prevailed, Athens would not have been enriched by the Garden of Epicurus or the Porch of Zeno.

Alexander's death at the age of 32 was a contingency which altered the course of history to an extent which it might be possible vaguely to conjecture if we knew what his immediate pro jects were. Unfortunately we do not know his projects. There is no good evidence for the popular idea that he was bent on the conquest of the whole world. It used to be thought that we had some genuine indication of his plans in a document known as his *Hypomnemata*.

But very recently Mr Tarn has shown convincingly that the *Hypomnemata* were a fabrication, so we have nothing like positive evidence to go upon. It is however certain that before his death Alexander must have been considering the future, and it would be natural that he should discuss his plans with his generals. We may therefore ask the question whether the ideas which Arrian (by whom the spurious *Hypomnemata* were not used) put in the mouth of Alexander (v, 26, 1-3) and in that of Coenus son of Polemocrates (*ib.* 27 , 7) were derived from material supplied in his principal sources,the Memoirs of Ptolemy and Aristobulus, or from the popular history of Cleitarchus. For, if from the former, it would be permissible to infer that three plans had been under consideration: (I) a new Eastern campaign to complete the conquest of India, (2) a northern expedition to Scythia and the countries round the Caspian, and (3) an extension of the Empire in Africa. What we do positively know is that since his visit to India the king had been much occupied with maritime questions. His admiral had made the sea voyage from the Indus to the Euphrates, and was preparing to attempt to circumnavigate Arabia and to establish a route by sea from Babylonia to Egypt. In the valleys of the Nile and of the Tigris and Euphrates, Alexander possessed two rich store-houses, like the Persians before him. But the Persians had allowed the cultivation of Egypt to fall into decay, and one of the most profitable tasks for its new king a task to which the Ptolemies afterwards addressed them selves with marked success was to renovate Egyptian agriculture and restore the productiveness of the land to its condition under the old Egyptian Empire. This would have been one of the first items in the economic organization of the Empire which Alexander must have undertaken. We know also that the situation in Macedonia was urgently demanding his presence. It seems therefore probable that be fore embarking on any further enterprises in the East, he would have returned to the West and organized Alexandria as a second capital And with his increasing insight into the importance of the sea, it is not a bold hypothesis that he would have aimed at establishing a thalassocracy in the whole Mediterranean. This would have meant the con quest of Carthage,and the conquest of Carthage by the Macedonian, who combined military genius and the command of immense resources, would have been no long task. So far we may go in our surmises, and if Alexander had done nothing more than that, the history of Rome, without its Punic Wars, would have been altered in ways we cannot imagine. A supposition of this kind is not idle. There is no sound reason for not recognizing, with Sir John Seeley, as legitimate and useful, the device of considering what might have been, in order to help one to realize the significance of what actually was.

None of Alexander's successors attempted to dominate the whole Mediterranean, an achievement reserved for Rome. Among the generals who fought over his inheritance, there were many of high military competence and some of uncommon political ability, but none had the sweep and power of their master's mind, no11e the spell of his personality. The only one who at all resembled him was Demetrius the son of Antigonus, who in military brilliancy might be compared *longo intervallo* to Alexander and had remarkable personal charm. But he had "some vicious mole of nature" in him, and he was not the man to rule an empire; he knew how to conquer, as Mr Tarn has said, but did not know how to govern.

Out of the conflicts which occupied many years after Alexander's death there ultimately emerged three great powers, each of which performed a different task, and while they were quarrelling over Greece, Syria or Asia Minor were all deliberately spreading Hellenism and unconsciously preparing the way for Roman dominion. The Antigonids of Macedonia were the protectors of the centres of Greek culture against the barbarians of central Europe who were pressing on the Danube; the Seleucids preserved Hellenism in the East and made the Parthians less barbarous; the Ptolemies prepared and set in order the store-house of Egypt which was to be Rome's richest possession.

It was the second Ptolemy who began methodically in the middle of his reign the operation of restoring the economic life of Egypt and making the soil yield all that it was capable of. By what methods this was done can be elicited from con temporary papyri and has been elucidated by Mr Rostovtsev in his masterly study *A Large Estate in Egypt in the Third Century* B.C. Ptolemy carried the work out as a landlord managing his own personal estate, during the last fifteen years of his reign, with the help of his trusted *dioecetes* or economic minister Apollonius, and ample remains of the correspondence of Zeno, who was the man of business (*oeconomus*) of Apollonius, have been preserved and supply rich information as to the lines which were followed in improving cultivation, irrigating sandy land, draining marshlands, constructing dykes, introducing viticulture, improving stocks, and organizing the administration. Mr Rostovtsev characterizes the work as a "systematic and logically progressive" exploitation of the resources of the country. It was carried out under the direction of Greeks,and its effects were durable.

All these Macedonian monarchs were champions of Hellenism; all of them, much as some might depart in practice from Hellenic ideals, believed devoutly that Hellenic culture was the most precious thing that humanity had produced. The Macedonians had fought for Greece in the Persian invasion and they had received as it were letters of naturalization in B.C. 476 when they were admitted to take part in the Olympian games. Though they were thus recognized as not barbarians, they continued to be regarded by the city states of Hellas as outsiders. Their political institutions differed and also their customs. The marriage of brother and sister, incestuous in the eyes of the Hellenes, was practised in Macedonia and the hellenized Macedonian monarchs never learned to consider it as abominable. Thus while Alexander's conquest meant the expansion of the Hellenic world, we must not forget that its rulers came of a state deeply differentiated from the cities which had a long tradition of Greek culture,and they were more capable of ruling successfully non-Greek peoples. It may be doubted whether any of the statesmen who made history in the old city states would . have been as successful in governing large heterogeneous kingdoms as were the ablest of the Macedonian despots. One characteristic of these kingdoms, which was distinctly Macedonian, was the considerable part which women of the royal houses played in political history, not on the whole a beneficent part, from Olympias to the last Cleopatra. Thee Stratonices and Laodices, Berenices and Arsinoes cannot be reproached either for cowardice or for scrupulousness.

It was only for about a hundred years that these monarchies, along with the small kingdom of Pergamum and some other minor states, went on their ways,little disturbed by what went on outside the Hellenic world. From B.C. 200 the shadow of Rome was imminent over them. Ptolemy Philopator and Attalus of Pergamum were perhaps among the first to realize that the future lay with the rising Western power. In the nineties of the second century, after the field of Cynoscephalae, it needed no Delphic inspiration to enable the poet of the *Alexandra* to speak of Rome's supremacy by land and sea

$$\gamma\hat{\eta}s \ \kappa\alpha\grave{\iota} \ \theta\alpha\lambda\acute{\alpha}\sigma\sigma\eta s \ \sigma\kappa\hat{\eta}\pi\tau\rho\alpha \ \kappa\alpha\grave{\iota} \ \mu\text{o}\nu\alpha\rho\chi\acute{\iota}\alpha\nu \ (\text{l. } 1229).$$

The story of the Roman annexations east of the Adriatic has been usually studied and usually told entirely from the Roman point of view. In order to understand Roman policy and judge it, we must look at it also from the point of view of the states that were its victims and observe events from Pella or Antioch or Alexandria or Pergamum as well as from Rome. Roman historians have procured currency for the view that Rome was involved in the politics of the Balkan Peninsula and Hither Asia against her will; that all her operations were entirely defensive, necessitated by the aggressive designs of the Macedonian states; that her con quests were the unavoidable and uncalculated result of measures which she was compelled to take in order to escape destruction; that her empire was neither desired nor designed but forced upon her. That was, no doubt, the perfectly sincere opinion of the generality of Romans. We have a modern parallel near home. It is probably the genuine opinion of many Englishmen that in the formation of the British Empire, English governments were never guilty of any aggressive purpose and were only forced by circumstances from time to time to take territories which they did not desire, either in self-defence or for the good of the world. But this is not a view which is accepted by other nations, who regard it as merely an expression of English hypocrisy. Rome's claim to be inoffensive and innocent of any desire for aggrandizement must have seemed singularly hypocritical to the despots whom she bullied and terrorized during the century after the Punic Wars. If we examine her acts and neglect the gloss she put upon them, we cannot help seeing, as Mr Bouché-Leclercq has seen, how perfidious the policy of her government must have seemed to the Eastern powers. In modern times, since the rise of democracies, despotic kings have not been greatly in favour, and it has been ex hilarating and edifying to see proud monarchs trembling at the word of a plain Roman who re presented a republic and disdained pomp and state; and in gazing on this admirable spectacle people have neglected the fact that the government of the Republic was an oligarchy as grasping and greedy as any of the majesties whom its consuls and ambassadors humiliated. It is needful to know not only the history of Rome herself but also the history of the Greek monarchs, and to realize not only her, but also their, political and social conditions in order to form a just view of her behaviour.

It must also be remembered that Rome was after wards confronted by the same problems that tested the abilities of the Macedonian rulers, when she took their place — such as the conciliation of central government with regional autonomy, the treatment of Oriental nations and of wild backward sections of mankind. She inherited their problems and she also learned from their solutions. In studying the Roman administration of Egypt or the exceptional position of many Greek cities under the early Principate, or even the way in which the earlier Emperors managed their financial business, we are inevitably led back to the methods of Alexander's successors. The deification of the Emperors is directly derived from the Macedonians; the device of maintaining a dynasty without sacrificing the elective principle, characteristic of the Roman Empire, was a Seleucid invention. To under stand the origin and nature of the *colonatus*, its latest historian takes us back to the landed estates in Ptolemaic Egypt.

It has I think been said that there was a certain , continuity in the traditions and fashions of monarchical courts, passing from the Ptolemies and Seleucids to the Roman Emperors, and thence coming down through the Middle Ages to modern times. Now there are certainly re markable re semblances between the court institutions of the Ptolemaic and Seleucid autocracies and the Roman autocracy into which the Principate passed towards the end of the third century, but the continuity through the intervening centuries of the Principate is not very apparent. I am disposed to think that the resemblances are due to a continuity, not in the West but in the East. The courts of the absolute monarchs of Egypt and Syria were strongly influenced by the Persian court of the Achaemenids, and the Oriental features which were adopted by Aurelian, Diocletian and Constantine,came from the Persian court of the Sassanids. It is a persistence of Achaemenid tradition through the Parthian period rather than a persistence of Seleucid tradition through the Roman Principate that accounts for the similarities which are noted between the Roman autocrats and the Macedonian autocrats. We may indeed say that the influence of ancient Persia in modern Europe has not yet been fully recognized. It is to be found not only in the general fashions and etiquette of royal courts, but also in the habits and traditions of diplomatic inter course. It was the relations between Roman Emperors and Sassanid monarchs that developed the strict conventions observed at Constantinople in dealing with foreign states and learned readily enough at other European courts,for in the Middle Ages Constantinople was in many ways the school of Europe.

It will hardly be contested that the considerations summarized in the foregoing pages supply good grounds for assigning to the period of the Macedonian monarchies a more leading and assured place in the study of ancient history than it has hitherto From been permitted to occupy.

the point of view of the progress of man, a great increase in knowledge of his environment or a great increase of his power over nature, has more wide-reaching effects and is a more signal landmark in history than any political changes. The invention of printing was a more important event than the Reformation, the discovery of the American continent more important than the con quests of the Turks.

In these respects our period is not an outstanding landmark in universal history; its interest is that it was on the verge of great discoveries, but came to an end without having made any absolutely decisive advance, or any momento us break with the past. It had its Copernicus; it had an explorer who has been compared to Columbus; but neither of them moved the world.

Aristarchus of Samos (active B.C. 290-260) demonstrated that the geocentric system of astronomy then in vogue could not be true as it did not explain the phenomena, and he hit upon the heliocentric hypothesis including the diurnal revolution of the earth round its axis. It was a flash of genius, and Aristarchus will always be remembered as the first man, so far as we know, who knew the general truth about the solar system. So far as we know ; for he may have been anticipated by some forgotten Babylonian savant. To be first with a scientific discovery seems to be as hard as it was to be first in getting into the pool of Bethesda.

But what happened to be the truth was not I received. The new theory must have made a certain sensation and it is interesting to find it denounced on religious grounds just as eighteen hundred years later, when it was revived by Copernicus, religious prejudices were one of the obstacles to its reception.

Of the philosophical schools which were acquiring such great influence in the third century, the Stoic was that which had most affinities with a religious community — it has been compared to a Church — and it was the head of the Stoic school, Cleanthes, who raised his voice against a man of science. The Greeks, said Cleanthes, ought to impeach Aristarchus for impiety for disturbing the hearth of the universe and dragging it to another place. The days were past in Greece for intolerance of this kind; in no age perhaps was the expression of opinion freer or rationalism more widely spread than in Hellenic lands in the third century B.C. The denunciation of Cleanthes could do no harm to Aristarchus, in fact it could only serve as an advertisement for his theory.

Why then in such an intellectual atmosphere was not the heliocentric discovery accepted ? Why did the leading savants of the following generations decline to entertain it? They were obliged to concede to Aristarchus that the current theory would not do, but they rejected his solution as too audacious. I am not sure, that they had not, as Mr Beloch has argued, a good case. This revolutionary theory, they might say, accounts for the observed phenomena; but otherwise there is no positive ground for any of the assumptions which it implies. If another hypothesis can be found that explains the celestial movements without disturbing the view that the earth is the centre of the planetary system, it deserves preference. And then the great , mathematician, Apollonius of Perga, came forward with the ingenious theory of epicycles which, leaving the earth undisturbed and comfortable in its old central home, seemed to furnish a full mathematical explanation of the movements of the heavenly bodies. This was the final word of Greek science and it prevailed unchallenged to the sixteenth century. When we remember that the Copernican theory did not convince a man like Lord Bacon, nor win general acceptance until the telescopic observations of Galileo confirmed it, I do not think we can blame the Greeks very much. They were on the verge of recognizing the truth, which if it had been recognized would have changed the history of the thought of the next two thousand years and produced incalculable effects. We may say that the judgment of the most eminent Greek mathematicians,

Archimedes, Apollonius, Conon, Hipparchus, decided a problem of vast importance for human progress and, as it turned out, decided it in the wrong way.

In the growth of man's acquaintance with the earth from the limited conceptions of the early Greeks to the full knowledge of the configuration of its lands and seas to which he has now attained, we may distinguish two Greek stages, and the time of Alexander the Great marks the beginning of the second. Both stages ensued directly from political movements; the first from Greek colonisation in the Western Mediterranean and the Euxine, the second from Alexander's conquests.

In the first period, the two most important steps were the invention of map-making by an Ionian philosopher and the epoch-making discovery that the earth is a globe, due to some Pythagorean man of genius. The study of geography never stood still from the time of Herodotus to that of Aristotle, and one result of observation and reflexion was to discredit the authority of the Ionian maps. Yet these maps continued in use down to the end of the fourth century. Then Alexander's penetration of the East as far as the Punjab and the voyage of his admiral, Nearchus, in the Indian Ocean, gave a new and powerful stimulus to the science of geography which the Greeks had founded.

And about the same time at which the eyes of the Greek world, amazed by Alexander's triumphal progress, were riveted on the East, new geographical facts were being gathered in the West in a region of which the Greeks were far more ignorant than they were of the Persian Empire — and gathered not as gleanings incidental to a military expedition, but as the fruits of the private enterprise of a genuine explorer who had no economic or political aims. Of Pytheas of Marseilles we know tantalizingly little. He sailed along the Atlantic coast of Europe,corrected old erroneous views as to the orientation of the coasts of Gaul and Spain, visited Britain and probably circumnavigated it, and re turning to the continent, travelled along the coast of the North Sea perhaps as far as the Elbe. He observed the noonday altitude of the sun at various places in these northern latitudes. One of his objects was to assist in solving what was one of the main problems of geographers at this time, whether the inhabited world is an island entirely surrounded by oceanic waters and what its shape is. The name of the book in which he recorded his discoveries is significant, *A Treatise on the Ocean*. It was published somewhere about B.C. 320; it was not known to Aristotle but was known to his pupil Dicaearchus. Greek geographers had known since the sixth century of the existence of Ierne, and of Britain under its oldest known name Albion, through in formation collected at Marseilles from Tartessian traders. Pytheas was the first to reveal to the Greeks roughly accurate facts about Britain collected at first hand. He has been described as "the Columbus of antiquity." He was not a rich man and what we should particularly like to know is under what conditions he mad his voyage from Cadiz and in whose ship. The Carthaginians who were masters at Cadiz did not encourage Greeks sailing in the Ocean.

But Pytheas never got the credit he deserved. He supplied data which were indispensable to the construction of a new world-map and Eratosthenes, the greatest of Greek geographers, seems to have recognized the value of his discoveries. Yet Dicaearchus, the predecessor of Eratosthenes, distrusted him, though he appears to have used him, and Polybius roundly declared that he was a liar.

The history of the geographical labours of the Greeks from Aristotle to Poseidonius is a difficult but fascinating study. One hardly knows whether to admire more the deductions of Eratosthenes, from the limited material available to him and the map which he ventured to construct, or the criticisms which his map evoked from the illustrious astronomer Hipparchus and the principles which *he* laid down for making a true map. Eratosthenes, working on the information furnished by Pytheas and the equally defective and possibly more misleading information that was available about the far East, was convinced that the oecumene or "inhabited world" was an island, and that the ocean around it was continuous. He thought that this was proved by observation except at two points, the extreme south and the extreme north, and that the chances that at those two points there was an isthmus of solid land were negligible.

He seems to have been misled by the confidence with which those who brought back reports from the East took it for granted that the East coast of India marked the eastern limit of the oecumene, and he accepted the statement of Patroles, that the Caspian was a gulf of the ocean in the north-east. It must be remembered that it was not till Roman times that anything appears to have been known about Further India and Cattigara (which may be Singapore). But inadequate as the grounds were on which Eratosthenes concluded that the oecumene known to him was surrounded by sea, immense as were the tracts of whose existence he had no idea, his general hypothesis was right, whereas the view of Ptolemy, who lived three centuries later, and knew in consequence of the Roman conquests far more geographical facts, and had the last word in ancient geography, his view that the Indian Ocean was entirely surrounded by land missed the mark.

Eratosthenes contemplated the possibility of sailing all the way in the same latitude from Spain to India if only the distance were not so great — he reckons it as over 13,000 miles and this was the view that prevailed till Columbus found the Western Oecumene. It was the view of Columbus himself, the view with which he started and indeed the view he held till his death, for he never knew that the lands which he had discovered were a new continent. But Eratosthenes only put forward this as one possibility. He also contemplated the pos sible existence of another or more than one oecumene in the Western Hemisphere. Which possibility he preferred we do not know.

The Greek geographers of the third and second centuries might have reached more accurate results had they devised and realized some scheme of voluntary cooperation or had the governments of the time given them active support. But cooperation in scientific research is a comparatively modern thing, though Hipparchus perhaps had a notion of it; and the successors of Alexander did not appreciate, as the Romans did, the practical value of maps. It is true that some of the Ptolemies promoted expeditions for the purpose of geographical discovery, but their interests extended only to the Red Sea, Ethiopia and the Ivory Coast, and to the Indian Ocean. The Seleucids did less than they might have done to promote the knowledge of Further Asia; and if Megasthenes and Deïmachus brought back some knowledge of Bengal, the missions on which they were sent to Palimbothra by Seleucus I and Antiochus I were political. The monarchs who inherited Alexander's dominions did not realize,as his imagination and genius had enabled him to realize, the importance of geographical work. He had Greek specialists with him whose business it was to record geographical observations, especially measurements of distances. These memoranda were carefully kept in charge of the royal treasurer, who after the king's death handed them over to Patrocles, the geographer to whom had been entrusted the exploration of the Caspian Sea and who succeeded (under Seleucus) in establishing the untruth that ' it was a gulf of the ocean. It is remarkable that on this point Herodotus had known the truth.

We may say on the whole that while the creation of geographical science by the Greeks is one of the eminent facts in the history of civilization, and while the study was prosecuted during this period with such notable success (due to the progress of mathematics as well as to exploration) that the period may I be called the great age of Greek geography,yet no discovery that could be described as revolutionary I was made in it, nothing comparable to the Pythagorean discovery .of the earth's spherical shape in the fifth century or even to the Ionian invention of maps in the sixth.

I must just signalize — I have not space to enlarge on — one other intellectual movement in the third century, which had a more permanent effect than the brilliant researches into astronomy and geography. It is well known. Philological science was founded at Alexandria, and systematic critical inquiries into the whole body of extant Greek literature began. The movement issued from the Peripatetic school — Aristotle was the pioneer in Greek erudition — and it was made possible by the foundation of the Alexandrian Museum, with its famous Library, of which the idea was due to the enlightened Peripatetic Demetrius of Phalerum when he was an exile from Athens under the protection of Ptolemy Soter. That was an event. Its consequences are written all over the world; we should not recognize our civilization if they were absent. Our public libraries, museums, academies of science and learning, universities have all a common parentage in the great institution which was under the patronage of the Ptolemies.

We may now go on to inquire whether any new original social idea was set afloat that influenced the course of civilization. The ideas which were particularly characteristic of the time and are most prominent, Imperialism, the divinity of sovrans, the legitimacy of absolute rule, were all important for the future, but none of them was new though they all entered on a new stage. But one idea then launched upon the world was quite new and was destined to control the future.

It has, I believe, been maintained that the word "barbarian" first acquired its depreciatory meaning in the fourth century, and from being a neutral term equivalent to non-Greek came to imply moral and intellectual inferiority. It is true that the idea of the inferiority of all non-Greek peoples to the I Greek was diffused and generally accepted in the Greek world in the fourth century but it certainly originated in the fifth. I think we may say with some confidence that the Athenians were responsible for the diffusion of this prejudice. We first find it in Attic literature or in literature directly under Attic influence. We find it very clearly in Euripides; for instance in the *Medea*, in the *Iphigenia in Aulis*, and especially in the Andromache. Thus in the *Iphigenia in Aulis* we meet the declaration that "It accords with the fitness of things that barbarians should be subject to Greeks, for Greeks are freemen and barbarians are slaves by nature." We find it also in Herodotus, and the evidence from Herodotus seems to be very significant. In the first six books, up to the battle of Marathon, the word occurs about a dozen times, and always in the neutral sense of non-Greek. In reading those books you can understand how an ancient critic blamed him for being philo-barbarian. It is only in the last books, written when Herodotus had come under Attic influence, that we find the word occasionally used with a derogatory implication, and constantly as a synonym for the Persians. We are, I think, entitled to conclude that the theory of the inferiority of the barbarians was started after the Persian Wars, probably at Athens, was propagated from this "School of Hellas," and became in the fourth I century a dogma accepted throughout the Greek world, firmly held by men like Aristotle and Isocrates. Xenophon, who had seen something of the wider world, was one of the few dissentients.

This belief of the Greeks in their privileged position among the peoples of the earth — which was as strong as the belief of the white races in their superiority to the coloured races to-day — lasted long after they had lost their political independence. They said, "We Greeks are great and good. As for the barbarians, they may learn from us but they must be kept in their place." Their eminent intellectual and artistic attainments, all they did for our own civilization, may prompt us in the account of the Ionic revolt "Persians" is always used, never "barbarians." to be indulgent to this self-exaltation; but the idea degenerated into an intolerant bigotry which a modern writer has considered a leading cause of their political decline.

There was born, however, in the generation after Alexander's death, another idea, sharply contrasted with this exclusiveness — the idea of mankind as one great community, the ideal of a state embracing the whole oecumene.

Zeno, the founder of Stoicism, established his school at Athens in B.C. 301 and taught for about forty years. Born in Cyprus he was a hellenized Semite. One of the things which his philosophy did was to overcome the distinction of Greek and barbarian. He introduced the idea of cosmopolitanism transcending patriotism; of the whole world, the oecumene, as a man's true fatherland; of a community embracing all rational beings, without regard to the distinction of Greek and barbarian, or of freeman and slave. According to this doctrine the philosopher feels himself citizen of a state to which all mankind belongs, a state whose boundaries are measured by the sun. In the ideal state of Zeno all human beings were citizens.

Now this idea was opportune; it came at the right time. It corresponded to the great revolutionary feature in the policy of Alexander, who in organizing his Oriental empire was bent on breaking down racial antagonisms and overcoming or softening the distinction between Greek and barbarian.(He recognized non-Greeks as part of the human family with equal claims on a common ruler.

The conception of a unity and fellowship of the human race did not do very much immediately to counteract the doctrine of the ingrained inferiority of those who were outside the Hellenic pale. It might be greeted as "a beautiful and inspiring thought"; but common sense was quite another thing. We may doubt whether this side of Stoic teaching made any appeal to such disciples as the Macedonian king, Antigonus Gonatas, who looked on Zeno as his spiritual guide, or to the Spartan king Cleomenes. The new idea did not help the plight of the native Egyptians.

But it was gradually propagated, and reached beyond Stoic circles. We hear that the great savant Eratosthenes, the librarian of Alexandria, whose geographical work has been touched upon above, censured Aristotle for advising Alexander to treat the Greeks as a leader, but the barbarians as a despot. Eratosthenes in his youth had been a disciple of Ariston of Chios, a heretical Stoic, who set up a school of his own at Athens. It may have been from Eratosthenes that Plutarch took the text for the passage in his *Essay on Alexander*, which associates the actions of Alexander with the doctrine of Zeno, a memorable passage which I will quote. Having enlarged on the civilizing work of Alexander, he says, "The much admired ideal of Zeno who founded the Stoic sect amounts to this: that we should not live in separate communities each with its own codes and laws, but that we should consider all men compatriots and fellow-citizens and that there should be one life and common order. Zeno put forward this as a dream or image of a state based on philosophical principles, but Alexander attempted to realize it. Aristotle had advised Alexander to behave to the Greeks as a leader but to the barbarians as a despot, treating the former as friends or kin but the latter as animals or plants. He did not follow that advice. He conceived that he was divinely sent to be the harmonizer and conciliator of Greeks and barbarians alike. He sought to blend as it were in the mixing-cup of good fellowship all civilizations and customs. He bade all men regard the world as their fatherland, not distinguishing Greek and barbarian by dress and outward appearance but making virtue and vice the criteria of distinctions among men." It is in Rome that we see this idea — the ecumenical idea, as I have called it elsewhere — bearing its earliest fruit. While the Roman upper classes had accepted from the Greeks the inferiority of the barbarians, from whom in assimilating Greek culture they dissociated themselves, they became familiar with Stoic doctrine, and it influenced the ideals of Roman administration, and the ecumenical idea dictated the claims of the Roman Empire to worldwide dominions.

Cicero says, in a passage of his *Republic* [1, 2], that the great motive for industry and toil among high-minded public men, is to increase the re sources — not (observe) of their own country, but — of the human race and to make the life of men in general richer and safer. Cicero was not a Stoic, and this passage illustrates how the Stoic idea of the community of the human race had penetrated ' beyond the professing members of the sect.

In the next century Pliny justifies the Roman Empire by its aim of providing one fatherland for all the peoples of the world. Its ideal was to be potentially conterminous with the inhabited globe, the *orbis terrarum*. Coming down three hundred years into the fourth century when the Empire was threatened by the Goths,we have Themistius praising (or defending) the magnanimity of an Emperor in not pressing too far his victory over the enemy,by an appeal to this idea. "You decided justly that even the barbarians ought not to be utterly destroyed because they also are really a part of your dominion, a complementary section of human kind. Therein you prove yourself a sovran of all the human race. No member of humanity is to be deprived of your care." But it is interesting to note how in the same breath the orator maintains the view of the inferiority of the barbarians.

Parallel to claims of the Empire and proceeding from the same origin was the claim of the Christian Church to be universal. In mediaeval theory the two claims were united. The passage I quoted from Plutarch strikes a leading note of the whole subsequent progress of man. For, apart from the in crease of his knowledge and power, has there been, any more salient feature in the advancing movement of human society than the linking up of all parts of the oecumene and the propagation of Western civilization, of which the foundations were laid in Greece, to all the margins of the world? In that movement Alexander took the first step. And in modern times the confederate idea of the solidarity and fellowship of the human race has be come an active and driving force. It has expressed itself as Internationalism which breaks down barriers and disowns country. It has expressed itself in the League of Nations. It is the intellectual basis of humanitarianism. It was Zeno who first taught men to think in terms of the oecumene.

Alexandrian Literature

IN one of the works of Walter Pater there occurs the following passage : —

The trial-task of criticism in regard to literature and art no less than to philosophy begins exactly where the estimate of general conditions, of the conditions common to all the products of this or that particular age — of the "environment" — leaves off and we touch what is unique in the individual genius which contrived, after all, by force of will, to have its own masterful way with that environment.

I will not venture to dispute the general truth of Pater's *dictum*, but in this lecture I have no intention of submitting myself to the test which he indicates. Dealing only incidentally with the separate appraisement of the various authors of the Hellenistic age, I wish to concern myself rather with what Pater regards as the secondary task of the critic, the description of environment and the fixing of general tendencies.

I chose this course for two reasons. Firstly, there are in existence several excellent studies of the individual writers of this epoch. Not to mention the general histories of Greek Litera- ture, we have in English Dr Mackail's *Lectures on Greek Poetry* which contains three chapters on the Alex andrian Poets; in French the brilliant book of Couat on the same subject; and in Italian the more recent work of Rostagni. My second reason is connected with considerations of time. It might be profitable to spend an hour in analyzing the characteristics of Theocritus or Callimachus or Apollonius Rhodius, but it would be mere waste of time to attempt the same task in five or ten minutes, and this is all that could be spared when there is so much to be said on the general outlines.

Even when thus circumscribed the subject to be treated in my lecture remains sufficiently large and only a selection of the facts can be given. The social and political background, for instance, must mostly be taken for granted and I shall only refer indirectly to such things as the rise of the vast Hellenistic monarchies with their mixed populations and their crowded capitals, or the great increase in wealth and luxury, or the foundation of endowed institutions of learning and the advancement of science.

By virtue of these things the Hellenistic world, it has been remarked, is in many respects nearer to the world of to-day than are the Greeks of the Classical Age. This is not merely true for the material background to life, but may be applied with equal justice to the age's attitude towards literature and the written word. Authors of every kind abounded, and the literary man, as a distinct type, is a creation of this epoch. From one end to another of the Mediterranean men were busy ex pressing themselves in writing ; on the other hand there was no lack of readers, since education was more widely if more thinly spread than in earlier periods. Further the mechanical production of "books" had been rendered easier and cheaper by the opening up of Egypt and its inexhaustible supply of papyrus to Greek industry and commercial enterprise.

Yet of all this literary activity there have survived down to our own day comparatively few examples. Prose has suffered much more than verse. Of the latter or at least of the most impor- tant school of it — Alexandrian Poetry — we have a reasonably large and representative amount, but the prose literature has perished almost entirely. There survives, it is true, a good deal of Hellenistic philo sophy and we still have much of the historian Polybius, but a consideration of these seems to be the concern of the lectures that follow — and in any case Polybius belongs rather to the Roman than to the Hellenistic period of Greek History. Deduct Polybius and the philosophers, deduct a few technical or semi-technical writers such as Euclid, and there is left nothing but an inventory of prose writers whose names may be found in the compilations of Susemihl and Christ but of whose works nothing or only the scantiest fragments still survive. It is a somewhat ironic stroke of fate that the gene rations which preserved and handed on to future ages the literary works of Classical Greece should have been unable to ensure the survival of their own writings, especially when those writings were to be numbered by thousands. But the reason for this disappearance of Hellenistic prose-literature is not far to seek.

During the first century of our era there was consummated a movement which had begun about the second half of the second century B.C. The Greeks definitely turned their backs on the literature of the Hellenistic age and demanded that in future writers should conform to Attic or what they deemed Attic canons. This *Renaissance*, as it is sometimes called, was retrospective as well as prospective; that is to say, not only did it lay down rules for the future, but it also applied these rules to the writers of the past and deliberately neglected those who offended against them. Such a standpoint was fatal to the survival of the Hellenistic prose-writers, for almost without exception these men were either careless of the form in which their thoughts were expressed or at the least quite unskilled in the graces and subtleties of the Attic style as understood by the Neo-Atticists. To take two outstanding instances, Epicurus' indifference to elegance of language is notorious and much of Polybius reads like modern journalese. It is true that the Hellenistic age produced its own characteristic prose-style, the so-called Asiatic, but the attempts in this direction were half hearted and in any case not unnaturally condemned by the later reformers.

These deficiencies of Hellenistic prose-writers are to be explained on various grounds. To begin with, Greek — the Greek of the $κοινὴ διάλεκτος$ — was now being written by many persons of non-Hellenic or at least mixed descent. The Semitic origin of several prominent Stoic philosophers has often been noted. Again the vocabulary of educated men had become enormously more technical. Someone has said that Plato had been able to construct a system without using more than one technical word. If we turn to Epicurus and the Stoics, we find that a whole vocabulary of technical terms must be learnt by heart before their writings become intelligible. It is true, no doubt, that in some ways an increase in technical terms marks an advance in thought (if it were not so, the twentieth century might well despair of itself!), but the habit among these writers goes far beyond what is necessary. Simple verbs are abandoned for compounds without any gain in expressiveness; abstract terms are found everywhere, and so on. After a short experience of writing, such as we find for instance in Polybius, we begin, I will not say to approve, but at least to understand, the reaction of the Atticists.

As a result of that reaction the bulk of Hellenistic prose has been lost to us: some books have survived because of their value for the specialist, many have been absorbed into later encyclopaedias and general histories, but many more must have simply perished. The loss is more important for the historian and scientist than for the student of literature, for, while it is extremely improbable that we have to regret the disappearance of any literary master piece, our knowledge of Greek History would be considerably increased, if we possessed — for instance — the Memoirs of Aratus of Sicyon, or Timaeus' monumental work on Sicily and Magna Graecia, or even Dicaearchus' account of Greek Civilization, entitled $Βίος Ἑλλάδος$.

Again much scientific and learned writing which would have been instructive and interesting has no doubt perished. As classical scholars we must desiderate with especial regret the works of Aristarchus and the other Alexandrian grammarians who devoted their lives to the elucidation of the Classics. It is, of course, true that fragments of their teaching remain imbedded in later Greek treatises — more particularly *scholia* — and from these modern scholarship has been able to reconstruct the main outlines, but many points must be left unsettled and nothing can replace the loss of the originals.

With this qualified tribute to the works which have perished we may leave the subject and turn now to the consideration of what actually survives. In this by far the most conspicuous element is represented by the writings which are known under the title of "Alexandrian Poetry" — owing to the relations which connected their authors with the Court, Library and Museum established by the Ptolemaic dynasty at Alexandria. The term is a convenient one and rightly calls attention to circumstances which certainly exerted great influence on many of these writers, but it must not be stretched to cover all the poetic output of the Hellenistic age. Recent discoveries of papyri have revealed to us the existence of a popular satiric and moralizing poetry which — in spirit at least — is quite alien from the products of the Alexandrians. Along with the two types just mentioned we shall do well to take into account what may be called the popular amusement-literature of the age, a mass of writing for which it is hard to find a comprehensive name but which may be loosely denominated as The Mime and its by-products.

As in the case of the popular moralizing poetry so in the case of the Mime our knowledge has been widely extended by the discoveries of papyri. This is not the place to dwell at length on the great services rendered by papyrology towards the illustration of the Hellenistic age, but the essential thing to remember is that before the advent of that science (and incidentally of the thorough investigation into the literary tradition which it has stimulated) our chief difficulty had been that we could not see below the surface. The history of the period, apart of course from Polybius, had to be gathered chiefly from late epitomes, and was then only a bare narrative of events. Now, thanks to the papyri, a great part of the legal and administrative system of Ptolemaic Egypt is laid I before our eyes. In religion, again, though it has been said that the Hellenistic age was the least religious in the history of the ancient world and though it is certainly true that a rationalism inherited from Ionia was its chief characteristic, nevertheless it is gradually becoming plain that we must not take the enthusiastic Pantheism of the philosopher nor the refined scepticism of the cultured poet as the faith of the average man. The research of Reitzenstein and others show us that the mystic Oriental cults which become so important under the Roman Empire were already in high favour with the populace. No doubt the ideas connected with these cults did not emerge into the higher branches of literature till the first century B.C., when Poseidonius made them familiar to Greeks and Romans alike, but their influence was felt long before.

The causes which have thus transformed our views of Hellenistic government and religion have not failed to affect literary criticism: the lower strata of Hellenistic literature begin to claim re cognition, and among these we can as I have said above, not unreasonably distinguish two tendencies — one represented by the moralizing poetry and one by the Mime.

Before we consider our three types of literature separately, it will not be amiss to say a word or two in explanation of their appearance at this juncture and regarding their inter-relations. When the Greek world began to settle down again after the conquests of Alexander, it certainly became necessary to create new types of literature, but we should err greatly if we supposed that the old fell into oblivion. While educated men had their libraries, public and private, the masses had their ἀγῶνες, i.e. public contests or competitions. The ἀγών, athletic or musical, had been one of the most important elements in the culture of classical Greece: among musical ἀγῶνες the most famous of course were the dramatic contests at Athens. As early as the end of the fifth century the Attic Dionysia were imitated in the islands and in Asia Minor. After the Macedonian conquests the institution spread far and wide over the newly-acquired territories. It is characteristic of the age that the athletic contests, now largely professionalized, were less popular than the musical. These latter might be either σκηνικοί or θυμελικοί, according as the performers appeared on the stage (σκηνή) or in the orchestra (θυμέλη): tragedies and comedies were played on the stage, while the other competitors, e.g. reciters of epic, panegyrists, musicians, etc., appeared in the orchestra. At the numerous new festivals, founded by the successors of Alexander in competition with the games of classical Greece, there were always ἀγῶνες of some kind, and it was customary to produce at them not only modern specimens of tragedy, comedy, epic, etc., but also works by the classic writers. The business of production and acting was managed by the so called "Dionysiac artists," troupes of professional players who were either permanently established in one city (Ptolemais, Rhegium, Syracuse, apart from many cities in Old Greece, are cases in point) or else wandered round from one town to another.

It is plain that in this way even the masses were still kept familiar with the ancient Epic and Drama.But when all this is admitted we must not take Theocritus' ironic Ἅλις πάντεσσιν Ὅμηρος as anything but the retort of a patron to an importunate poet. If educated men, as represented by the Alexandrians,were not content with their in heritance, neither were the cosmopolitan inhabitants of the new royal towns — "the Macedonians who had degenerated into Syrians, Parthians,and Egyptians" as Livy scornfully styles them. Both classes were thrown back on their own resources with the result that the cultured took refuge in "art for art's sake," in the pursuit of curious learning — and in the cultivation of a mild sentiment for romance. On the other hand the lower classes consoled them selves with the farcical and humorous, and with the frankly sensual — features which one or other of the various types of Mime was able to supply. The moralizing poetry and prose of the Hellenistic age come in as a kind of counter-blast to the two tendencies just indicated. They are directed equally against the superficiality of the erudite poet and the sensuality of the proletariat — more perhaps against the former than against the latter, for they are closely connected with the Cynic philosophy, and the Cynics were always more charitable to primitive than to civilized vice. Ethical considerations of this kind are unknown both to the Alexandrian Poetry and to the Mime. Eratosthenes, a fair representative of the Alexandrian school — though he was more *savant* than poet — objected to moral criticism of Homer, and Alexandrian Poetry as a whole — with the possible exception of Aratus — disclaimed any moral or religious mission. It was the same naturally enough with the Mime. But while the latter on this point ranges itself with the learned poetry in opposition to the moralists, in one feature, viz. its realism, it quits the Alexandrians and joins the other side. For while the learned poets, owing to their taste for *genre* treatment, were wont to practise a curious realism in details, their general tone, on account of their subject-matter and almost as it were in spite of themselves, was distinctly romantic and idyllic. The Mime on the other hand was naturally dominated by a realistic spirit, while as for the moralists one has only to read Diogenes Laertius' *Lives of the Cynic Philosophers* to learn that few people have believed more firmly than they in calling a spade a spade.

It is amusing to observe the very different handling of the same theme by the Alexandrians on the one hand and the mime-writers or moralists on the other. Two instances will show what I mean. To take the first. Diogenes Laertius in his *Lives* has recorded many scandalous details about the private life of the various early philosophers. This "information" or much of it has been traced to an anonymous book, entitled Ἀρίστιππος περὶ παλαιᾶς τρυφῆς, which was apparently written between 250 and 200 B.C. The author was a Hedonist of some sort or other and his object was to show that the principles which he advocated had actually been put into .practice by the founders of philosophy. The pseudonym *Aristippus* was no doubt chosen with reference to the founder of the Cyrenaic school of Hedonism. Many of the stories which this pseudo-Aristippus records can be traced back beyond him, and against his treatment of them we may set that of an Alexandrian poet, Hermesianax of Colophon, who lived one or two generations earlier. Athenaeus has preserved a long fragment from the third Book of Hermesianax' *Leontion*, a curious work in which the poet set out to teach his mistress, after whom the poem is called, that all the great men of the past had felt the force of love. Towards the end of the fragment Hermesianax catalogues the love-affairs of the philosophers. Pythagoras, Socrates, and Aristippus are mentioned, and though, as poetry, the passage is distinctly feeble stuff, there is a certain air of tender melancholy about it which some modern critics appear to have found attractive.

The lines on Socrates and Aristippus run as follows :

> And you know with what mighty fire wrathful Cypris melted the heart of the sage proclaimed by Apollo to be the foremost of mankind in wisdom — even Socrates, and how going constantly to the dwelling of Aspasia he relieved his profound mind

of pain and lightened his burden, nor yet could he find any remedy, though he had
found many a path through argument. Desire too it was that drew the man of
Cyrene to cross the Isthmus what time keen-minded Aristippus fell in love with
Lais and fled from all converse with his fellows....

Comparing Hermesianax with the author of the περὶ παλαιᾶς τρυφῆς we see the gulf which
separates the two.

. Another example of different handling of the same theme comes to light in regard to
the Assyrian monarch Ninus, who in the verses of the moralizing poet, Phoenix of Colophon,
figures as the type of the dissolute tyrant, but in an early prose romance found in Egypt appears
as a manly hero and the honourable lover of a modest princess.

So much for the general tendencies and inter relations of our three types of literature. It is
time that we turned to consider them separately.

Of the Alexandrian poetry there have come down to us in the ordinary way the *Hymns* of
Callimachus — the *Argonautica* of Apollonius Rhodius — Theo critus — three didactic poems
(one by Aratus and two by Nicander) — the *Alexandra* of Lycophron — and a considerable
number of epigrams by these and other writers. Under the circumstances this is much, though
the selection contains no real specimen of the Alexandrians' most important and characteristic
composition — the narrative elegy.

The Attic Renaissance interfered but little with the preservation of Alexandrian poetry: the
archaizing tendencies of the latter appealed to the Stylists, while its obscure allusions and difficult vocabulary commended it to the professional scholars, the παῖδες γραμματικῶν as Clement
of Alexandria calls them. That we possess no more of it to-day seems to be due to accident,
for some works such as the *Aitia* and *Hecale* of Callimachus can be traced right down to late
in the Byzantine period.

As a result of this survival through the Roman and early Byzantine ages we have, in addition
to the complete works catalogued above, a very large number of fragments cited from Alexandrian poets by grammarians and others. Unfortunately only a very few, like that of Hermesianax
quoted earlier, are long enough to be appreciated. To this inheritance transmitted by the usual
channels the discovery of papyri has added Herodas and a good deal of Callimachus' works other
than the *Hymns* and *Epigrams*, including a portion of his *Aitia* which is of great importance for
a just appreciation of Alexandrian achievement and its limitations.

That achievement is too often said to lie exclusively in its attention to and mastery of poetic
form. This defect of criticism seems to be due to the fact that these poets have usually been
considered chiefly in relation to their Roman imitators, and that in this connexion it is certainly
correct to emphasize the *formal* importance of the school. But this accident ought not to blind
us to the real nature of the facts: if we look beyond the Romans to certain productions of
Greek literature under the Empire, to Nonnus and his school, to the Greek novelists, to the
letter-writers, Alciphron and Aristaenetus, or even if we examine a little more closely the short
epics (epyllia) of the Roman νεώτεροι, (Catullus, Cinna and the rest), it becomes plain that
the Alexandrians, besides being masters of form, were also very important innovators in poetic
material.

I do not refer here to the "didactic" poetry of Aratus and Nicander, nor to the thousand
and one odd subjects, which an enterprising age clothed in metrical form. Many of these "didactic" writers are simple *metaphrasts*, that is to say, they do nothing but take a prose treatise
and turn it into verse. It was in his way that Aratus versified the astronomical treatise of Eu-
doxus and Theophrastus' remarks on weather-signs; similarly Nicander in his *Alexipharmaka*
and *Theriaca* is versifying the prose-writings of one Apollodorus — on "Antidotes to Poisons"
and "Snake-Bites" respectively. The works of Nicander are but little mentioned in antiquity, but
the popularity of Aratus is one of the puzzles of literary history. Astronomy is no doubt a fitting
subject for poetry, if adequately treated, but Aratus makes no attempt to soar. A mild Stoicism
pervades the poem, but it may be doubted whether this fact explains the appeal which Aratus

made both to Greeks and Romans. The only thing which to-day really merits our admiration in these poets is their ingenuity in putting technical terms into verse. This ingenuity is greater in Aratus than in Nicander, for it is more difficult to suggest in verse the shape of an isosceles triangle than to depict in the same medium the results of drinking white lead.

Again when I speak of innovation in poetic material I do not even refer to the Pastorals of Theocritus and his imitators. These of course have exerted a very great influence on succeeding literature, but they do not reveal, except incidentally, the essence of Alexandrian Poetry. This must be sought rather in its relation to and treatment of mythology.

Ever since the dawn of Greek history the mythology of the epic cycle had supplied the material for nearly all Greek poetry — epic, lyric, and tragic. But times were now changed, and amid the literary war-cries which issue from the school of Callimachus, we find expressions of dislike and contempt for those poets who still pursue the beaten track. That this opposition to the so-called "cyclic" writers was not directed merely against their unimaginative repetition of Homeric phraseology seems to follow from passages where Callimachus reveals his distaste for the *matter* of the epic cycle. But, if the heroic mythology was to be regarded as exhausted for poetic purposes, to what could the poet turn? Sheer invention was unnatural to the Greek turn of mind; nor was the choice of a strictly historical theme looked upon with much favour, since it limited the poet's freedom. Hellenistic monarchs sometimes maintained court poets, whose duty it was to sing their patrons' achievements — one such was the epic poet Simonides of Magnesia, who celebrated the victories of Antiochus Soter — but though, if we may judge them by the official panegyrics of Theocritus and Callimachus, these poets wrote with more grace and less servility than the Roman eulogists of the Caesars, their reputation was not great.

Nevertheless, though no inspired writer appeared able to fashion current history into a great epic, the historical had much interest for these *Epigoni*, and in their search for new poetic material they tried to combine something of the old mythology with the history or pseudo-history fashionable in their own age. It must not be supposed that this fusion was due to the Alexandrians: we should always remember Callimachus' words of warning — ἀμάρτυρον οὐδὲν ἀείδω. As a matter of fact the material lay there before them, with the mythological and historical elements already combined, but waiting to be touched into poetry. It was to be found in the Local Legends, the myths, that is, explanatory of local custom and ritual which, scarcely touched by the Homeric influence and Athenian tradition, still survived in the places which had given them birth.

In Asia Minor and more especially in Ionia these myths were still vivid in the minds of the people or carefully treasured in the city annals. Ionian influence on Hellenistic civilization has long been recognized: exactly then as the Ionian dialect influenced the κοινὴ διάλεκτος so the spirit of Ionian literature affected the tendency of Alexandrian Poetry. For these tales and local legends were selected by the Alexandrians as material for poetry, and in this selection lies perhaps the greatest importance of the school.

The famous quarrel between Apollonius and Callimachus has tended to give undue prominence to the Callimachean ideal of polished brevity, and to make modern critics, as perhaps also contemporaries, almost forget that, though their temperaments were very different and though in consequence the spirit which colours their writings is dissimilar, yet in one respect Apollonius and Callimachus were in agreement. If not altogether in his *Argonautica*, at least in his other poems Apollonius like Callimachus turned from the highway of Homeric saga to the themes of local history and mythology. The other poets of the age did likewise.

The greater number of these stories are narratives of unhappy love, either between two mortals, or between a mortal and a god or goddess. Many of the latter kind are attached to a locality by the "metamorphosis" idea, i .e. the belief that some , stream or rock or what-not in the neighbourhood really represents the shape assumed by a maiden fleeing from the amorous god, and so on. In the former class a favourite theme is the princess in the besieged city, who betrays her folk to the enemy out of love for the commander of the besieging army: the Italian story of Tarpeia, the subject of an elegy by Propertius, the Roman Callimachus, is perhaps the most famous of all tales of this description. No doubt in many of these stories there is a nucleus of historical fact, but in course of time the particular has been obscured by the typical.

Our chief source for these tales is the mythological handbook of Parthenius. Parthenius was a Greek of Nicaea in Asia Minor who was brought captive to Rome somewhere about 75 - 70 B.C. and became instructor of the poets (Calvus, Catullus, Cinna and the rest) who were attempting to build up stricter canons of style by a close study of Alexandrian poetry. Parthenius himself has been called, not without reason, "the last of the Alexandrians." He was also the teacher of Virgil and it was for Virgil's friend, the poet and politician Cornelius Gallus, as he tells us in the preface, that he put together this collection of love-stories, for that is what his book calls itself. Ἐρωτικὰ Παθήματα. Gallus was to use the stories as the material for his epic and elegiac poems, and here we may be sure that Parthenius is recommending the practice of the Alexandrians.

In the single MS. of the Ἐρωτικὰ Παθήματα, attached to most of the tales, is a brief list giving the names of authors who have recorded them. These lists, it has been proved, do not always give the sources used by Parthenius himself, but they are generally regarded as trustworthy and as the work of some accurate and widely-read scholar of comparatively early date. A perusal of them is instructive: along with the names of Alexandrian poets such as Apollonius and Euphorion, we find frequent mention of local historians, e.g. *Aristocritus in his History of Samos, Aristotle and the Historians of Miletus*, and so on. Besides Miletus and Ephesus I other districts which seem to have been fertile in such legends are Bithynia, Pallene, and the islands of the Aegean.

Before the Hellenistic epoch not many poets, so far as we can see, had exploited the material contained in these legends. Stesichorus, the early Sicilian poet, was perhaps the first to introduce the theme into literature, but his *Kalyke* and *Rhadina* found no immediate successors. The Athenian tradition was unfavourable to the motive, though here, as in so much else, Euripides foreshadows the taste of later generations. Ovid, it is true, can write of Tragedy

haec quoque materiam semper amoris habet,

but that was much later, when Alexandrian influence had affected even drama. It is more to the point perhaps to observe the changed attitude which historians later than the Attic age adopt towards these legends. Thucydides had made but a passing and contemptuous reference to the story of Tereus, Procne, and Philomela: on the other hand writers like Timaeus and Phylarchus seem, to judge by the fragments, to have been at great pains to develop any episode of this kind which crossed their path.

The way was thus paved for the Alexandrians, and to some extent their choice of material must have been influenced by contemporary taste, but two particular reasons may be adduced to explain that choice. The first is simply their position as writers attached to an.establishment of learning, the Museum at Alexandria. Being as much scholars as poets they turned very naturally to ξέναι καὶ ἄτριπτοι ἱστορίαι such as the local legends. Further a more immediate influence was probably exerted — at least upon the earlier Alexandrians — by Demetrius of Phalerum. Whatever the part played by this person in the foundation of the great Library at Alexandria, it is certain that during the earlier period of Alexandrian Poetry the Peripatetic school was the leading school of philosophy in the Egyptian capital, a fact that is plausibly attributed to the influence of Demetrius. But not only had Aristotle and his successors shown more ardour than the other schools in investigating the psychology of love, they had also distinguished themselves by their researches into local history and constitutions. Studies like these must have brought to light plenty of poetic material, for in nine cases out of ten the overthrow of a τυραννίς was connected with some episode of passionate love.

The second reason which accounts for the treatment of these stories by the Alexandrians is the rejuvenescence of local patriotism. This phrase may seem paradoxical in view of the tendency to cosmopolitanism which admittedly marks the Hellenistic age, but by "local patriotism" in this context is to be understood not a living faith in a country's present, but a sentimental enthusiasm for its past — in other words just such a feeling as produced so many local chronicles of the Ἀτθίδες type about this very time.

Some cities had no title to fame except in their legendary associations. Thus both Strabo and Mela tell us t hat Sestos and Abydos contain nothing of interest except the tower of Hero and the story of Hero and Leander, and in the same connexion it has sometimes been suspected that the late Greek poem by Musaeus on this subject is based on an earlier Hellenistic original, which made the tower and its obscure origin the starting-point of the narrative. Ancient cities such as those just mentioned were alive to the material advantages which the glories of their past might procure for them: they seem to have run a Publicity Department and we get a glimpse of its methods when we read inscription s which mention the rewards given to poets for singing the past of this or that city. These complimentary poems were known as ἐγκώμια ἐπικά, and were generally recited at the ἀγῶνες θυμελικοί. In many cases we find the services of a distinguished writer employed for this purpose, and poems which narrated the foundation (κτίσις) of cities became a recognized branch of Alexandrian art. Apollonius for example wrote κτίσεις of Rhodes, Caunus, Alexandria, and Naucratis besides a poem called *Canopus*. When we reflect that Apollonius, who was almost certainly a native of Alexandria, subsequently received the citizenship of Rhodes and perhaps of Naucratis, we begin to understand that these poems were not written in the air. Th ere were practical reasons which tended to draw the interest of the Alexandrians to local legend.

In what ways did they handle their material? The departments of Classical Greek Poetry may be put at five, viz. epic, lyric, elegiac, tragic, and comic. Hellenistic Comedy had best be considered with the Mime and of the remaining four two need not detain us long, for lyric was practically dead and tragedy was in not much better plight.

In the first half of the third century B.C. certain Tragic poets were known as the *Pleiad*, and seem to have enjoyed considerable fame among their contemporaries. We can form but little idea of their achievement. One member of the *Pleiad* was Sositheus, who is praised by a writer in the Anthology for having revived the ancient coarseness of the Satyric Drama — a doubtful compliment. Another was Lycophron, the only Hellenistic tragedian of whom we possess a complete drama. This extraordinary monologue-play — the *Alexandra* can scarcely be representative of contemporary tragedy nor perhaps is it typical of Lycophron himself, for that he could write lighter verse, when he chose, is shown by the fragments of his Satyric drama, in which he pokes fun at the philosopher Menedemus and the coterie of intellectuals at Eretria, among whom the author had spent his youth. His versification in the *Alexandra* of obscure mythology, which is mostly taken from the geographer and historian Timaeus, accords with Alexandrian principles, but Lycophron lacks the qualities by which such poets as Callimach us redeemed their works from dulness.

Lyric, we have said, was practically extinct. Songs continued to be written for public festivals and processions, and both Callimachus and Theocritus attempted lyric measures, but in Alexandrian poetry these are exceptions. Poetry was now written, if not for reading, at least for recitation, so that it came to be composed almost exclusively in the three metres which adapt themselves to recitation — the hexameter, the elegiac and the iambus. It is significant that Theocritus modernizes Pindar and Stesi chorus by rewriting their lyric compositions in hexameters. Iambic metres — especially the scazon or choliambic verse — were frequently employed in the Helle11istic age, both by the Cynics and others, as we shall see, for moralizing poetry and by the Alexandrians for informal miscellaneous writing, mildly satirical, such as we get in Callimachus' *Iambi*, of which work a largish fragment has been discovered among the papyri from Oxyrhynchus.

But the two metres chiefly favoured by the Alexandrians were the hexameter and the elegiac. The hexameter was used for epic compositions such as the *Argonautica*, for the shorter works called ἐπύλλια, for the pastoral, for hymns, and many other subjects. The elegiac could also be adapted to hymns, but was chiefly employed for narrative elegy and every kind of epigram. The material derived from local legends seems to have been usually treated in either ἐπύλλια or narrative elegies. Of a real Hellenistic ἐπύλλιον we possess no satisfactory example, but we can form some idea of the genus by separating the third Book of Apollonius' *Argonautica* in which he describes the love of Jason and Medea, from the rest of the poem, or again by reference to Roman imitations such as Catullus' *Peleus and Thetis*, the *Ciris*, or Book IV of the *Aeneid*. As regards narrative elegy it is true that we possess no complete specimen even of this, but we have considerable remains of the *Apollo* by Alexander Aetolus, the *Leontion* by Hermesianax, the *Erotes* by Phanocles, and the *Aitia* by Callimachus. Compared with the imitations of the Romans and later Greeks these remains enable us to judge with some confidence of Alexandrian achievement in this branch.

Our point about the importance of the local legends has been that their exploitation by the poets meant the introduction to Greek Poetry of romantic and erotic motives which had not hitherto been given adequate presentment. Unfortunately most of the Alexandrians were prevented alike by temperament and environment from making the most of the opportunity which offered itself. It is perhaps possible here to make a distinction between the first and second generation. Some of the former, though in style they are genuine Alexandrians, wrote before the full effect of the close connexion established between poetry and learning at Alexandria had made itself felt. Philetas and Hermesianax, following in the steps of Antimach us of Colophon, who lived a generation or so before them, seem to have kept their narrative love-poems fairly clear of irrelevant learning, but in the later Alexandrians the romantic interest is made subordinate to the aetiological.

The fragment of Callimachus' *Aitia* discovered at Oxyrhynchus is very instructive on this point. By a rare stroke of good fortune it contains part of the most celebrated episode in the whole work, the love-story of Acontius of Ceos and Cydippe of Naxos. The tale is well known from Ovid's *Heroides* and other sources, how Acontius by a ruse obtained from Cydippe an oath that she would marry him, how her parents in ignorance tried to wed her to another, with the result that Cydippe invariably fell ill on the eve of the marriage, how eventually Apollo at Delphi enlightened Cydippe's father and all ended happily. Callimachus' handling of this story in the *Aitia* had been largely reconstructed, before the discovery of the new fragment, from the adaptation in the late Greek letter-writer Aristaenetus. When compared with the latter, the fragment from Oxyrhynchus shows how Aristaenetus with his rhetorical training has infused into the narrative a pathos which is notably absent from the original. It now appears that Callimachus merely happened upon the story when he was putting into elegiacs the prose chronicle of Ceos compiled by one Xenomedes. He tells us this in so many words himself, and he records the chequered career of Acontius and Cydippe with no more enthusiasm than that which he devotes to various points of early Cean history that are treated immediately afterwards. The poetry is brilliantly superficial: Callimachus makes no attempt to analyze the sentiments of the two lovers or to do anything but record the facts. In short there is a complete absence of humanity.

In view of this it is disconcerting to find that the ancient world seems to have regarded Callimachus' presentment of this tale as the ideal love-story. We are left wondering, but we may note this. Some of its popularity may have been due to its happy ending. Most Alexandrian love-stories — see Parthenius *passim* — concluded in much more tragic fashion: the metamorphosis motive in particular rarely permitted a happy ending. In his tale of Acontius and Cydippe Callimachus hit the popular taste and it was this type of story — i.e. of two lovers first kept apart by all manner of difficulties, but afterwards united — which eventually won the day and centuries later inspired the Greek Novelists. Only a small part of the credit for all this is due to Callimachus and his fellows: they had stumbled almost by accident on first-rate poetic material, but they had bungled in their use of it. The plain fact is that the Alexandrians had little heart, arid all the cleverness in the world could not compensate for this deficiency.

The exception proves the rule. For Apollonius of Rhodes whose portrayal of Medea in his *Argonautica* is the greatest piece of character-drawing in Alexandrian poetry, was reckoned a heretic by his contemporaries and it has been shrewdly suspected that it was this revelation of humanity and a genuinely romantic spirit and not some academic difference of opinion concerning the merits of long and short poems — which really brought about his quarrel with, Callimachus.

In this connexion it is extremely difficult to explain why the Roman elegists so constantly refer to the Alexandrians — especially Philetas and Callimachus — as their masters in the art of amatory poetry. The love-elegy as we find it in Tibullus, Propertius, and Ovid seems to have little connexion with narrative poems such as the *Aitia*. It has therefore been argued that Philetas and Callimachus at least wrote not only narrative elegies in which stories like that of Cydippe found a place, but also subjective erotic elegies in which they described their own affairs of the heart much in the manner of the Roman poets. The alternative theory is that the Latin subjective elegy dealing with love was a more or less original product, a development and enlargement of the Greek amatory epigram. The problem remains and must remain undecided, but it is certainly true that what genuine feeling and passion the Alexandrians possessed they seem to have reserved for their epigrams. There is nothing in the more ambitious works of Callimachus which from this point of view can equal the famous memorial verses on his dead friend Heraclitus.

The Greek epigram has a long history before the Hellenistic age, but it was the Alexandrians who fashioned it into an instrument marvellously adapted to convey their comment on every aspect of the life that surrounded them. Of the extant Hellenistic epigrams the greater number are amatory, and these, though they already employ all the conventional machinery of artificial love-poetry, e.g. the boy Eros, his arrows, and the rest of the paraphernalia, nevertheless, at least in the hands of poets who stand rather outside the Museum circle, such as Asclepiades of Samos, still exhibit a genuineness of feeling which under the circumstances is perhaps surprising.

Our two remaining types of Hellenistic writing, the amusement-literature and the moralizing poetry, may and must be treated more briefly. Both exhibit popular elements which are absent from the works of the Alexandrians. Their appeal was primarily to the masses and in the case of the amusement-literature this appeal was made not through books — the day of cheap novels and the comic press had not yet dawned — but through the spoken word of public performances.

The same thing is, of course, true for Athens of the fifth and fourth centuries, but Athenian tragedy and comedy, the vehicles of popular education and amusement in those centuries, were ill adapted to serve the same purpose in the Hellenistic age. Tragedy, as we have seen, continued to be performed, but it can scarcely have appealed to the crowd. The same remark applies even more to comedy. The art of Aristophanes could convey little meaning to a subject of the Ptolemies and even the New Comedy with all its cosmopolitanism was only at home in the academic and rather supercilious Athens of Hellenistic days. It is true that the Ptolemies made some attempt to persuade the leading writers of the New Comedy to desert Athens for Alexandria, but Menander refused the invitation and even Philemon, who accepted, stayed only a short time. It is obvious that the atmosphere was uncongenial. There is however one exception and that not without significance. Machon, a native of the Peloponnese and the author of comedies, is expressly said by Athenaeus to have resided in Alexandria and to have exhibited his plays there. These have not survived: but from another work of the same man, viz. a witty but somewhat obscene collection of anecdotes relating to *hetairai*, Athenaeus has preserved for us considerable extracts. Compare these with the writings of Menander and the other authors of the New Comedy, who are careful to preserve at least a semblance of respectability,and the difference between Athenian and Alexandrian taste is revealed.

The inclination of the masses in the Hellenistic age was towards realism, to a close study and representation of the life which surrounded them, a life which, owing to increased luxury and the mingling of nationalities, had become more sensual than that of their predecessors, and this inclination found satisfaction in the Mime, which according to the definition of an ancient grammarian is "an imitation of life embracing both what is proper and what is improper."

Certainly in this period and probably afterwards there were two kinds of Mime, one spoken and one sung — the actors being called μιμολόγοι and μιμῳδοί respectively. The two varieties probably originated in different parts of the ancient world, the spoken Mime being a native of the Doric West, and the Mime which was sung of the Ionian East. There are obvious re-semblances between the culture and civilization of Magna Graecia and Ionia on the one hand and of the monarchies of the Diadochoi on the other. In the earlier period there are great cities, e.g. Syracuse, Miletus, Ephesus, which anticipate the various capitals of the Hellenistic age, and life in these cities was almost as complex and luxurious. It was therefore natural that a type of art, which seems to have arisen amidst this early city-civilization, and then to have suffered temporary eclipse during the age of Athenian supremacy, should regain its popularity when the former conditions of life were largely reproduced.

The spoken Mime, then, originated in Magna Graecia, being probably a development of one of the forms of "Dorian Comedy" imported from the Peloponnese. Such a development would not have been difficult, for there is evidence that even in the Peloponnese "Dorian Comedy" could eschew mythological travesty and its phantastic elements and concentrate on the realistic portrayal of life. Athenaeus, at least, tells us of a dramatic entertainment at Sparta called the *Deikelon* in which the actor represented (ἐμιμεῖτο) such different characters as a fruit-thief and a foreign doctor. Apart from the literary Mimes of Theocritus and Herodas the only specimen of a spoken Mime which has survive belongs to a considerably later period, but there is plenty of evidence for the popularity which these works enjoyed in the Hellenistic age.

Even as early as the fifth century B.C. Syracusan performers began to wander East, exhibit-ing their skill in the mimic art. But it was only about the beginning of the third century B.C. that, thanks no doubt to the increasing unity of Mediterranean civilization, the actors of mimes became as regular a feature of the Greek world as the other travelling players. Produc-tion was apparently in the hands of the vague class known as θαυματοποιοί and the ordinary troupe probably included no more than three or four persons. Of these practically all except the ἀρχίμιμος were of negligible importance, for the Mime was essentially a one-actor affair. To begin with, no doubt, this was literally true, but later the original actor took in certain complementary persons as the occasion required — e.g. if the ἀρχίμιμος were acting the part of a doctor he would require a patient and so on — but he always contrived to retain all the threads of the action in his own hand. The importance of these "actor managers" is well illus-trated by the epitaphs of *archimimi* — and by those of *archimimae*, for — another advance in realism — women appeared in the mimes no less than men, in fact, to judge by the remains, even more frequently. Thus it would appear that by the third century B.C. the Mime had obtained an adequate class of players, though naturally the less ambitious nature of their plays and perhaps the inclusion of actresses — no doubt women of ambiguous morals — caused the Dionysiac artists to regard them with suspicion. From forming a mere side-show to the dis-plays of Tragedy, Comedy, etc. they gradually pushed their way into the official programme at games and other festivals. As early as 270 B.C. θαυματοποιός Cleopatra is mentioned in an inscription of Delos among other prize-winners, and from this date onward μιμολόγοι βιολόγοι, ἠθολόγοι (all names denoting the actors of spoken Mimes) appear with increasing frequency in this connexion.

So much for the external features of the spoken Mime. What of its content? Here the task of the literary historian is rendered difficult by the lack of material. We have,as noted above, one Mime from Oxyrhynchus: this papyrus belongs to the second century A.D. but the com-positions which it contains, a Mime and a Farce, are assigned to late Ptolemaic or early Imperial times. We have some hints in Athenaeus, which all tend to show that the subject matter of the Mime was taken from low life, and lastly we may within limits argue as to the nature of the popular Mime from the literary type composed by Sophron, Theocritus, and Herodas.

The theme of the Mime from Oxyrhynchus is the same as that treated by Herodas in his fifth Mime, to wit a jealous mistress and a slave who refuses to yield to her demands. The details of the action remain obscure and it is probable that the papyrus contains merely the outline of a play jotted down as the basis on which the company could improvise as they pleased. The coincidence with Herodas has been variously interpreted, some thinking that the work from Oxyrhynch us is a popular adaptation and expansion of the earlier composition, others supposing that both mimes are handling a traditional subject independently.

Of Mimody, i.e. of the Mime which was intended to be sung, we possess more examples than of the spoken Mime. Improvisation was here more difficult and consequently the words of a piece were more likely to be written down from the beginning. Mimody, we have seen, derives from Ionia, and the performers are to some extent degenerate rhapsodists. Thus, while the actors in the spoken Mime probably appeared in everyday costume and without masks, those in the musical Mime wore a long white garment and a golden crown. Festus defines one of-the two chief types of the mimode as *lascivi et delicati carminis cantator* and no doubt the ordinary productions of Mimody *were* of this description, like the "Ionian songs" referred to by Aristophanes and Lucian.

The papyri have preserved several examples of this variety of the Mime. By far the most important is the famous *Alexandrian Erotic Fragment.* This is not really a fragment at all, but a complete composition which gives the lament of a deserted *hetaira* who pleads outside her lover's house to be taken back again into his affections. The piece is written for the most part in excited Dochmiacs: the language is the κοινή of the second century B.C., set off with many poetical expressions. There are obvious resemblances between this composition and the second Idyl of Theocritus. Only here we have a vehemence of phrasing and a wild licence of the emotions which are absent from Theocritus.

Another example of Mimody has been found inscribed on the wall of a rock-tomb at Marisa in Palestine. Its contents are a striking confirmation of a passage in Athenaeus, where he tells us that all Phoenicia was full of the so-called "Locrian" songs, which are, he says, songs with adultery for their theme.

We are told by Aristoxenus that Mimody was divided into two types — hilarody and magody, the former being a burlesque of Tragedy and the latter of Comedy. If this is correct, the Farce from Oxyrhynchus mentioned above is a specimen of hilarody, for it is a parody of the story made famous in Tragedy by Euripides' *Iphigenia in Tauris.* A Greek maiden, Charition, is held captive by Indian barbarians: her brother succeeds in rescuing her after making the Indians and their king too drunk to follow in pursuit. A realistic feature is that the barbarians are represented as speaking their own language, which has been identified by Orientalists as one of the dialects of Southern India.

Before concluding this section of our subject it seems necessary to say a word about the literary Mimes of Theocritus and Herodas. Both these Alexandrian writers were fallowing in the tracks of Sophron, the father of the literary Mime, who flourished about 450 B.C. and wrote at Syracuse. It is impossible to reconstruct any one Mime of his from the fragments which survive, but the titles, e.g. "The Tunny-fisher," "The Messenger," "The Sempstresses," "Women Spectators at the Isthmian Games," etc. show that Sophron was concerned to depict typical scenes from everyday life. There was no phantastic element such as remained in Athenian Old Comedy, no parody of mythology like that practised by the other great Sicilian, Epicharmus, and, revived in the third century by Rhinthon and the various authors of *Phlyakes.* The Mime in the hands of Sophron was simply an imitation of life. In one respect Sophron stood nearer to the non-literary Mime than his imitators did: he wrote in prose — a "rhythmical prose" it is true, whatever that may mean, but prose for all that. When Theocritus and Herodas composed their Mimes in verse, they were definitely sacrificing one instrument of realism. Of the two Theocritus with his hexameters naturally idealizes more than Herodas with his scazons.

Of Herodas' Mimes we possess seven, with considerable remains of an eighth. The pieces bear out the definition of the Mime which we cited earlier, for Mimes 1, 2, 5, and 6 all deal with rather unpleasant subjects. But Herodas is never offensive: his art is purely impersonal, and he shows neither anger nor pleasure in regard to his characters. The only subjective note is one of ironical depreciation.

Theocritus has left us three Mimes, viz. Idyl II (*The Sorceresses*), Idyl XIV (*The Love of Cynisca*), and Idyl XV (*The Syracusan Women*). All three have long been recognized as masterpieces of inspired realism. His Bucolic Idyls have sometimes been classed as Mimes dealing with rustic life, but here Theocritus idealizes far more than in the urban Mimes and deliberately omits much that a more realistic handling of the theme would have been bound to include. Yet it should be noted that his procedure is by no means the same in all the bucolic poems. Least artificial are without doubt Idyls IV and V; in these the scene is laid in Magna Graecia, and it is a reasonable theory that they represent Theocritus' first essay in the portrayal of rustic life, an essay made early in his residence at Cos before the vivid impressions of a boyhood spent in Sicily and Southern Italy had faded away. Next to these in realism comes Idyl X; the remainder are far more artificial. Either Theocritus generalizes and sublimates his subject as in Idyl I, or he uses the Pastoral as a setting in which to place his friends and contemporary authors. Idyl VII, the famous *Thalusia*, is admittedly the best example of this so-called "Bucolic Masquerade," but there are in addition other poems where the intention is the same if less obvious. In Idyl XI, for instance, the picture of the love-sick Polyphemus and the parody of motives dear to the writers of the amatory elegy is surely a satire not so much on contemporary poetry, as is sometimes supposed, but on a fashion or affectation of contemporary life. But Theocritus' satire is always friendly and f good-natured, perhaps because it springs not from any moral earnestness but simply from his strong 1 sense of humour.

The debt of Herodas and of Theocritus in the urban Mimes to Sophron is hard to estimate. Some verbal resemblances are striking, but it is absurd to talk as though Theocritus had done nothing but modernize the earlier writer. Both he and Herodas used their own eyes and described , contemporary life from their own observation.

Our last type of Hellenistic literature — the productions of the moralists and the satirists — has been described above as a kind of counter-blast to the unmoral poetry of the Alexandrians and the immoral pieces of the variety-stage. As might be expected its authors have no connexions with the Court and Museum of Alexandria: satire and moralizing were not appreciated by the Ptolemies, as Sotades drowned by the royal Admiral for his attacks on the private life of Ptolemy II found out to his cost. Most of the moralists spent their lives roaming about the Greek world: if they settled anywhere it was at Athens where the population tolerated them as harmless eccentrics just as it had tolerated Diogenes in the fourth century. Priding themselves — to the point of ostentation — on their independence they viewed with contempt the scholars and poets penned up in the Museum of Alexandria — an institution which one of them, Timon of Phlius, described as "the hen-coop of the Muses." The scholars returned the attack, if it be true that it was Eratosthenes who described Bion the Borysthenite — perhaps the most famous among these wandering moralists — as having dressed philosophy in ἄνθινά, the coloured garments of the courtesan, or in other words of having prostituted that noble science. Theocritus with his gibes at the starved and ill-kempt devotees of Pythagoreanism voices the same dislike. Bion was θεατρικός, i.e. he played to the gallery, said his critics, and such methods were abhorred by Alexandrianism.

The prose form in which these men usually expressed them selves seems to have been that which it is fashionable nowadays to call the *Diatribe*, a type of literary composition which is very variously defined by different scholars. Ordinarily by this term is meant the pagan equivalent of the Christian sermon, a popular homily on some familiar theme, delivered by an itinerant philosopher to such audience as he can collect at a street-corner, or in some camp or at a public festival. These harangues appear to have been marked by certain features of style which would appeal to the mob, e.g. antithesis, personification, metaphors, puns, etc. I suspect that

German scholars have attributed to the Diatribe virtues which it usually did not possess: at any rate the moralizings of Teles who is supposed to reproduce Bion — the so-called founder of the Diatribe — are platitudinous to the point of dulness.

But the prose Diatribe is far too complex a subject to discuss here. We can only consider — and that briefly — the satirical and moralizing works which were composed in verse, or in the medley of prose and verse of which Menippus of Gadara was the chief exponent.

There are perhaps five writers in this department of whom we are able to form a more or less adequate idea. These are Crates of Thebes, Menippus of Gadara, Cercidas of Megalopolis, Phoenix of Colophon, and Timon of Phlius. Of these five the first three professed adherence to the Cynic philosophy, but Phoenix can not be shown to belong to any school, and Timon was a Sceptic, a follower of Pyrrho.

That the Cynics were the chief representatives of popular philosophy in the early Hellenistic age may be admitted, but in recent years there has been an obvious tendency to exaggerate their importance. Every scrap of moralizing which can be assigned to the third century B.C. is asserted to be of Cynic origin and books are written to prove the all-pervading influence of the Cynic ideas in later literature. It is certainly true that the paradoxes of Antisthenes and Diogenes had become widely known by 300 B.C. and that they afforded a useful basis for any would-be satirist or preacher. Further the school could still boast many notable representatives in the third century, but the other philosophic systems contributed not a little to the development of the literature which we are considering, and in addition there was a large body of popular moral teaching which owed nothing to philosophy but had been simply handed down from one generation of ordinary men to another. The general colour of the Cynic ideas is well known. Marked features of their system are its transvaluation of ordinary values, its criticism of society its exaltation of the poor and oppressed. Clearly these are ideas of which the satirist and moralist can avail himself without difficulty, and in fact the Hellenistic writers whose inclination was this way did so avail themselves, but they were not all for that reason Cynics.

It may seem strange perhaps that men like Crates and the other writers just mentioned should have employed verse for the exposition of their ideas, but several considerations may be put forward to explain this phenomenon. To begin with, one of the most favoured instruments employed by these men to inculcate their ideas was Parody, and Parody naturally tends to be parody of verse. Again, it was the fashion to regard early Greek poets like Archilochus and especially Hipponax as in some ways the precursors of the popular preacher of the third century, and the scazon metre of the latter was constantly used by Hellenistic moralists, no less than by learned poets such as Callimachus. Lastly, though in some ways it was an age of prose, it was nevertheless a time when the field was free for any kind of poetical experiment, and at such a time it would have been strange if philosophy alone had escaped being put into verse.

Crates of Thebes is an interesting figure, a man of possessions who abandoned them to embrace the life of a wandering philosopher and thus became the first Cynic missionary, for Diogenes, his Master, seems to have been little more than a notoriety hunter. Crates on the other hand was inspired with a genuine zeal for conversion, anxious to "labour with men" (in John Woolman's pleasant phrase) for their soul's good, and earning the nickname of θυρεπανοίκτης from his habit of making house-to-house visits. His literary works are like the man himself, simple and homely but possessing a certain straightforward charm. He wrote, it appears, tragedies, παίγνια (parodies in the hexameter and elegiac metre),and letters. Crates is the first Cynic parodist and set an example which his successors were not slow to follow. One form of parody, the so-called *Silloi* poems, in which Homeric lines and phrases were employed for the purpose of a more or less personal satire,had already been made famous by Xenophanes in the sixth century and was soon to be revived by Timon. A few lines of Crates which survive show that he too had written such poems. But this Hellenistic Quaker scarcely possessed the qualities which satire of the kind just mentioned seems to demand: he was more at home in quiet parodies of every variety of verse, in which he was able to correct the mistaken standpoint of his originals, or supply a moral if none existed. His most famous effort in this direction was his parody of

Homer, entitled *Pera* (*The Wallet*), in which this outward symbol of the Cynic faith gave its name to a sort of Utopia. Among the fragments the following two lines are notable for their expression of a sturdy independence:

ἡδονῇ ἀνδραποδώδει ἀδούλωτοι καὶ ἄκναπτοι
ἀθάνατον βασίλειαν ἐλευθερίαν τ᾽ ἀγαπῶσιν.

Menippus of Gadara was a very different person. Of the man himself we know little, amounting to n0 more than this, that he was the slave of one Baton in Sinope, later became a pupil of the Cynic Metrocles and having amassed a fortune in commerce died a freeman of Thebes. This somewhat drab if respectable career forms an odd background to his writings so far as we can reconstruct them. He appears in the handbooks as the creator of the σπουδογέλοιον type of literature, the mixture that is of the earnest and the jesting, the aim of which is *ridentem dicere verum*. "A mocker of man's ephemeral existence" Marcus Aurelius calls him; "A terrifying hound with a treacherous bite" says Lucian in the passage where he confesses his debt to him.

The works of Menippus are lost, but fortunately he had imitators in plenty both Greek and Roman, among them Varro, Seneca (in his skit on Claudius) and Lucian, and from these writers it is possible to win some idea of the original which they all followed. Lucian is our most helpful source, and for this reason. It would appear that after the Atticist Renaissance Menippus was forgotten by the Greek world till Lucian discovered this discarded jester who was a compatriot of his own and modernized, that is, "Atticized" him to suit the prevailing taste. In two passages Lucian openly admits his debt, but recent research has shown that the later writer's originality was even smaller than was supposed. Many points naturally remain open to doubt, but it does seem possible to reconstruct in outline at least one composition of Menippus — his Νέκυια. In this work, which was really rather a Κατάβασις or *Descent into Hell*, he described how he visited the Lower World in order to find Teiresias and to ask him which is the best life. Here on earth the philosophers all preach different creeds and Menippus ironically pretends that certainty can only be reached in some such supernatural way as this. He finds the blind seer in the end and receives his answer that the best life is the life τῶν ἰδιωτῶν, by which he seems to mean a life exempt from any kind of dogmatism, and the wisest policy τὸ παρὸν εὖ θέσθαι, a response which Menippus might have given himself without the trouble of visiting Hades. But of course the Teiresias-motive is a mere framework into which is set the vision of what Menippus saw in the underworld. The description of this seems to have fallen into the usual inconsistencies, which are almost inevitable when a writer is dealing with such a theme; but two motives stand out above the rest, firstly a bitter ridicule of the rich and of des potic rulers, and secondly a parody of the serious works which narrated the Descents into Hell of Orpheus, Heracles, and the rest, and a caricature of all theories which terrified man with pictures of t a world beyond the grave.

Menippus seems to have employed many other settings for his caustic satire — banquet scenes, as cents into heaven, auctions and so on; but Lucian's imitations do not allow us to distinguish the original so well as in the case of the Νέκυια It is clear that Menippus had a marked gift for satire: he spares no man, and though he professes the Cynic creed he has no mercy for others who professed it without sincerity. His main object no doubt was to display his nimble wit: the moral influence of his writings was a minor consideration, and from this point of view one may compare him with Diogenes rather than with Crates.

Cercidas, our third Cynic moralist, has of course only emerged from obscurity since the publication of a papyrus from Oxyrhynchus which contains substantial fragments of his *Meliambi*. A successful politician in third century Greece, he was in intimate relations with Aratus of Sicyon during the latter's attempt to combat the communist and revolutionary tendencies brought into existence by the economic crisis of those days. But despite these relations Cercidas professed to belong to the Cynic school and there is evidence in the fragments that he was not blind to the justice of some of the claims put forward by his political opponents. In the longest of these according to the most likely interpretation he first satirizes the habits of the niggard and the spendthrift, then questions the existence of a Divine Providence, and concludes by warning his fellows of the wealthy class that unless they mended their ways and showed more charity to those below them, they would be caught by the full blast of the Social Revolution and compelled to disgorge all that they possessed. Of the remaining fragments one is more autobiographical: in it Cercidas addresses his soul and contrasts his own placid expectation of old age and death with the usual reluctance of men to close their eyes on this world. The other pieces for the most part deal with less pleasing aspects of the Cynic creed, such as their Hedonist conception of Love and so on.

Phoenix of Colophon is another writer rescued from oblivion by the papyrologists. His editor has made manful efforts to claim him as a Cynic, but it does not appear that he was a whit more affected by Cynic ideas than any man who wrote in that age as a popular philosopher was bound to be. His scazons exhibit some skill in phrasing and a certain effectiveness of vocabulary, but his subject-matter is not of great interest, being for the most part commonplace moralizing on the failings of the rich and the undeserved sufferings of the poor. Still to-day he is the chief representative of what must once have been a considerable body of writing in which standards very different from those of the Alexandrian Poets were applied to Hellenistic life.

A far more interesting figure is Timon of Phlius. Timon was in his philosophy a Sceptic, a follower of Pyrrho of Elis, but he was no ordinary philosopher. Like King Antigonus he possessed but one eye, but unlike the monarch who refused to have his portrait painted till an artist hit upon the brilliant idea of painting him in profile and so invented a fashion, Timon boasted of his own infirmity and was never tired of referring to himself as Cyclops. Born at Phlius he was first a stage dancer, then a successful sophist practising for long years at Chalcedon, finally a teacher of philosophy living for the most part at Athens and Thebes. His moral character might seem to be impugned by Diogenes Laertius who calls him φιλοπότης (fond of the bottle), but Wachsmuth in his edition of the Sillographi shows, I think, that the text does Timon an injustice and that the more eulogistic word φιλοποιητής (a lover of poets) should be substituted. Timon was like the leading Cynics a "character," and Antigonus of Carystos, the biographer of the philosophers, described him as ἰδιοπράγμων (an independent sort of person). He was quick at observing men's weaknesses, say the records, and an adept at turning them to ridicule. Other stories picture him as the abstracted sage who allows his writings to lie about half-eaten by the mice. To the same trait may have been due his omission (duly noted by Diogenes) to take any breakfast, though Wachsmuth would regard this as asceticism. Timon was a man of considerable learning: his knowledge of Homer is shown to have been great by the skilful way in which he parodies the epics, and we are told that Aratus the poet consulted him on the question how to obtain the best text.

Of his prose-writings two only are known to us at all clearly, viz. the Πύθων, in which he recorded his conversion to Scepticism, and the Ἀρκεσιλάου Περίδειπνον (*Funeral Feast of Arcesilaus*), a sort of palinode in which he atoned for the attacks that he had previously made on the same man. In the verse-writings the satiric intent is more obvious. Diogenes gives a formidable list, viz. tragedies, satyric plays or perhaps comedies, *iambi* (?), and — most important — *Silloi*. Nearly all the surviving fragments come from these last. Whatever the derivation of the word Σιλλός, it implies a poetry of which the chief ingredients are ridicule and invective. The style originated, as we have seen, with Xertophanes in the sixth century, and a generation before Timon seems to have been employed by Crates. Timon followed in the footsteps of Xenophanes, but like most satiric writers of his age, e.g. Menippus, added considerable elements from Comedy, for instance a passion for monstrous compounds, an affectation which he shared with Cercidas. In his *Silloi* Timon's aim was to satirize the dogmatic philosophers and he realized this purpose by a parody of Homer in which the Epic phrases were perverted to expose the weaknesses and exaggerations of the various pundits, and in which whole motives, e.g. battle scenes, visits to the lower world, etc., were adapted for the same object.

In his satiric outlook as in his vigrant life Timon shows himself in sympathy with the Cynics, but in one particular he was very un-Cynic. The *Silloi* is emphatically not a popular poem. To appreciate the satire it was necessary to possess a pretty comprehensive knowledge of the history of philosophy, and it was no doubt to give readers this knowledge that in later ages two scholars at least wrote commentaries on the poem. Thus though Timon sneered at the academic society of his day, the inmates of the Alexandrian Museum, his chief work must have been as much "caviare to the general" as was the poetry of the learned poets.

The main purpose of this lecture has been to suggest that the conventional view of the Greek writing produced in the Hellenistic age is somewhat one-sided. The tendency of that view has been to stress the "learned" character of the literature belonging to this epoch. Operating in the main with the works of the scientific prose-writers and the Alexandrian Poets and judging the latter rather on the form than on the content of their writings, rather in relation to Rome than to later Greece, critics have been misled into drawing a picture of Hellenistic literature which was too consistent to be accurate. The researches inaugurated by Rohde in his illuminating book on the Greek Novel have shown that even the Alexandrians bequeathed to posterity something more than the art of writing "learned" poetry brilliantly: on the other hand the Egyptian discoveries of the last forty years have brought to light two other types of Hellenistic writing which contrast sharply with productions of the poets attached to Court and Museum. These two popular types are animated by a realistic spirit, while the learned poetry, in virtue of "its material, exhibits incomplete but undoubted inclinations to romanticism.

Th e connecting-link between the Alexandrian Poets on the one hand and the Mime and Moralizing Writers on the other is to be found in such writers as Theocritus and Herodas, who handled the popular material according to the principles of Alexandrian art. The realism which, to a different degree of course, governs the work of the two poets just mentioned and which also appears with good effect in such compositions as the epigrams of Leonidas of Tarentum, dealing as these do for the most part with humble life, is found sporadically in more conventional works of the Alexandrians, where its appearance is somewhat incongruous. Callimachus it is true in his *Hecale* seems to have given a charming picture of the old woman who entertained Theseus prior to his encounter with the bull of Marathon and of her rustic cottage, but the ordinary Alexandrian use of this motive was more artificial. The learned poets delighted to depict the life of the gods and heroes in all the detail which they observed in the life of men. Sometimes the gods are described as living in the everyday fashion of the ordinary mortal, some times in that of a Hellenistic king or princess. Instances of the second kind are Apollonius' description of Eros and Ganymede playing at dice like two court pages, of Aphrodite at her toilet-table, or Theocritus' picture of Ptolemy Soter and Alexander conducting Heracles to his sleeping-chamber — "when he hath taken his fill of fragrant nectar." For the first sort we have Callimachus' interesting anecdote about Hermes and the daughters of the gods, how, when they are naughty, in collusion with their mothers he disguises himself as one of the Cyclopes and rushes out of the house to terrify them into obedience. Similar in kind are Theocritus' careful studies in the youth and upbringing of Heracles, or in the household arrangements of Alcmena and Amphitryon.

Touches like these seem to suggest that even the Alexandrians were not wholly uninfluenced in some of their ideas by the more popular tendencies of the age, but the difference of standpoint between them and the other writers is far from being bridged by coincidences such as these just noted. Nowhere does that difference emerge more clearly than in a passage of Horace's *Satires* where he first translates an epigram of Callimachus on the typical Alexandrian theme of the love which

καὶ φεύγει φιλέοντα καὶ οὐ φιλέοντα διώκει,

and puts it into the mouth of his romantic lover, and then asks in language reminiscent of Diogenes or Cercidas, how pretty verses such as these can do anything to cure the torments and disorder of the soul:

Hiscine versiculis speras tibi posse dolores
atque aestus curasque graves e pectore pelli?

The indignant question might well stand as the verdict of the Hellenistic Moralists on their Alexandrian contemporaries; but there is no need why it should be ours as well. However much we may be compelled in the light of the new discoveries to revise our notions about Hellenistic literature as a whole, Alexandrian Poetry will still retain its importance and interest, not so much perhaps on account of its own achievement as for the sources of inspiration which it revealed to later writers. To take one instance out of many — Ovid, except for Alexandria, could scarcely have written his *Metamorphoses*, and not only modern literature but modern art as well would have been the poorer for the loss.

Hellenistic Popular Philosophy

THE Macedonian conquest of the Nearer East marked a great epoch in human history. In the preceding centuries a culture of peculiar quality had been developed in the Greek city states which possessed the southern part of the Balkan Peninsula and tracts of sea-board in other parts of the Mediterranean Sea. That culture had already, when Alexander set out to attack Persia, produced the great works of literature and art which we study to-day as classical. Through the Macedonian conquest there came a great change. Hellenic culture had been generated and focussed in the frame of the city state, and if we cannot say exactly that the frame was now broken, it was at any rate depleted, depotentiated, when large numbers of the citizens of the old Greek cities were drawn away to populate the new cities in the East and when all Greek cities, old and new, had their scope of political action restricted by the predominant power of one or other of the new Greco-Macedonian royal houses. It has often been described how the individual Greek, under the changed conditions, found himself much more of a loose atom in a world of vaster geographical horizons. In the old days the life, political and social, of his native city had given the ordinary man all the interest he required; its traditions and public opinion gave him something of a moral code. But now its politics had become parochial by comparison with the larger world and failed to supply adequate interest, whilst outside in the lands thrown open to commercial enterprise, in the courts and armies of Hellenistic kings, were new possibilities of excitement, adventure and the acquisition of wealth. In the markets and courts and armies Greeks from a multitude of different city states were indiscriminately mixed together, not a stable society with fixed traditions, but crowd of individuals, each out for his own profit in the great scramble. A world of unrest, the Greek citizen *déraciné*, unrooted, with no end in life but to get wealth, to get sensation, to get power — disorder and giddy chance in the place of the regular activities, amenities and duties of the old city state, a society demoralized as all societies must be in which there are continual dramatic vicissitudes of fortune, the same man now on the pinnacle of power and riches, now flung down into the mud. There was no sense or principle or order in the course of things, it was just a huge haphazard play of chance, of luck, Τύχη, the only deity to be discovered in the world.

But, of course, there were many people to whom such a world could not give permanent satisfaction. The hunting after riches and after sensation might fill life with interest for a time, but inevitably it produced often the reaction of a great weariness and disgust. Men who felt themselves whirled along in a confused dance came to long for some firm rule of life. The ancestral Hellenic religion, although it certainly had a moral element in it, although no doubt the idea that the gods, the powers ruling the world, were on the side of righteousness, was still to some extent alive — the Hellenic religion was so mixed up with baser elements, at any rate with crude and primitive elements, that it could not supply such a guide as the Hebrew had in the Law of Jehovah. It was in these days that philosophy, which did purport to supply a guide, became popular as it had never been before.

Philosophers were to be seen everywhere — in the streets of the cities, at the banquets of kings, — Platonic, Peripatetic, Stoic, Epicurean, Sceptic, Cynic, those of the ascetic schools being assimilated to the humbler lass of manual workers in their dress — the plain sort of mantle called a *tribön*, whilst philosophers generally were marked out, in a society where it was the rule for men of the upper class to shave clean, by the long beards which they were commonly believed to cherish with care and pride. Between the rival schools controversy was always going on, and it tended often to become violent. Lucian gives us vivid pictures of the wrangling and scuffling between philosophers in his time, the second century of the Christian era. But even in the earlier Hellenistic time we may see in Diogenes Laertius how bitterly the philosophers of different schools often attacked each other. Philosophers contended for the souls of kings. A curious document in this connexion is the life of the Epicurean philosopher, Philonides, deciphered a few years ago in a papyrus roll from Herculaneum. This man was a contemporary of the Seleucid king, Antiochus Epiphanes, the "little horn" of the book of Daniel, notorious for his attempt to Hellenize the Jews by force. Philonides went to the Syrian court to convert Antioch us to Epicureanism, for Antiochus at the time apparently professed himself a believer in the rival Stoic creed. He was now plied with Epicurean tracts. We are told that after the king had read, or Philonides had read to him, no less than a hundred a11d fifty tracts, the good work was done and Antiochus embraced Epicureanism.

Whilst however these quarrels of philosophers are evidence that there existed sensible differences between the schools, perhaps what most strikes one to-day in going over the remains of that voluminous ethical literature which they severally put forth, is the extent of that which all the schools had in common. The ideals of temper and conduct which governed that ancient world, so far as men sought at all to rise above mere sensuality and greed of gain, were embodied in a kind of popular philosophy, much of which might have come from any of the rival schools. We may say that the aim which they all set up for the individual to strive after was expressed in the word αὐτάρκεια, self-sufficiency, independence. The horrible thing, so it seemed those days, was to be caught In the rush of this universal unrest which had no end or issue, to be whirled along helpless like a stick in a torrent, at the mercy of chance, Τύχη, Fortuna, at the mercy of one's own spasmodic desires. If the movement of the world, in which the individual finds himself involved, has no perceivable purpose, if there is no cause larger than himself which he may hope to see go forward, and go forward in some degree by his own devotion and efforts — then for certain men there comes, sooner or later, an imperious desire to escape from the current, to find rest for the soul in some firm standing-place outside the turmoil. For some temperaments the continued excitements and pleasures of the world may keep up interest, may maintain a kind of intoxication which never allows this desire for emancipation to assert itself; but for other temperaments the cry for freedom arises with an urgency which will not be denied. It was to men in this mood in the Hellenistic world that philosophy came, to show them the way of deliverance. Why were they entangled in this unrest, dragged hither and thither by forces outside their control? The answer was to be found in the I distribution of interest. Every interest man had in any object was a filament, as it were, going out from his heart and attaching itself to that object, so that if the object was unstable and elusive he was pulled miserably after it. The way of freedom therefore was to cut all these strand going out all directions and attaching to a multitude of objects, to abolish interest in everything except in — but at this point the schools diverged. They were all agreed that deliverance was to be found in reducing the field of interest; but they were not agreed as to the object upon which interest should be concentrated.

Most of this popular philosophy of the Hellenistic and Roman world, whether uttered upon the air of the streets or embodied in little rolls of papyrus, has perished for ever from the memory of men, but we may see a specimen of it in the extracts from the sermons of Teles preserved for us by John Stobaeus. Teles, of whom we know nothing except from these extracts, seems by internal evidence to have belonged to the middle of the third century B.C. and to have drawn largely from the written discourses of a much abler man, Bion of Borythenes — the far-off Greek colony in the Crimea. Bion was the cynic preacher, of whom Eratosthenes said that he was the first to clothe philosophy in gaudy raiment ($\mathring{\alpha}\nu\theta\iota\nu\grave{\alpha}$ $\mathring{\epsilon}\nu\acute{\epsilon}\delta\upsilon\sigma\epsilon\nu$). There was something theatrical about his style, and he drove home his satire by trenchant, often coarse, colloquialisms. Teles too apparently followed the Cynic way — the sect which went farthest in denying values ordinarily recognized by the citizens of Greek cities. The ordinary man's life was largely governed by his attachment to possessions of various sorts, to certain kinds of food and to good clothes, to a particular place — his native country — to particular people, his children, for instance, and friends. It was this attachment which brought all the trouble into his life and made him dependent on circumstances outside his own control. The Cynics point out the way of securing independence by a simple abolition of interest in these things. Possessions? Why, rich men don't actually use a large number of the things they possess. And what profit is it then to possess them? They have such things only in the sense in which a banker possesses someone else's deposit (p. 26). The slave gets on well enough without someone to wait on him; why should a free man be any less independent? Many poor men, Aristides, for example, have been more honoured in their cities than any of the rich (p. 36).

Food? The roads are full of herbs and the springs of water. Look, says Teles, at those old women singing in their quavering voices as they munch a common barley-cake (pp.4, 5). You can buy a quart of lupines for a copper coin (p.9). You don't need a kitchen of your own to fry your couple of sprats. The bronze-founders will no doubt let you use their furnace (p. 30).

Good clothes? In cold weather there is no need to seek a thicker mantle. You have only to fold your present old cloak and there you have a garment of double thickness all ready (p. 30).

Native country? What of substantial worth does the exile lose? I am excluded, you may say, from the governing body of citizens in a strange city. But how many people in your own country are excluded from the governing body — women, slaves — and do not make a grievance of it? As for the disgrace of banishment, if you were banished, although virtuous, the disgrace is theirs who banished you, not yours (pp. 16, 17).

Fellow-citizens? In the present war, says Teles — that is, probably, the Chremonidean war (265-261), it is the rich man who is troubled by having to think about others; the man who has attained freedom by having no dependents is in the happy position of having to think about no one but himself (p. 36).

Children and friends? If the free man is not going to be worried about his own death, why should he be worried by the death of his children and friends? "How unreasonable and utterly foolish for a mall to sit weeping and mourning because his friend is dead! Making himself ill as well! If he is really going to act according to the values of this mad world, it would seem to be more philosophic for him to grieve whilst his friend is still alive, reflecting that his friend will have to die some day. It shows a strange perversion of judgment, as Stilpo said, for a man to stop thinking about the living for the sake of those who are here no longer. That is not the way the husbandman behaves. If one branch of a tree dies, he doesn't lop off the others as well, but t ends them with extra care, so that they may replace the branch that is gone. Because my son or my wife is dead, is that any reason for my neglecting myself, who am still alive, and ceasing to look after my property?" (p. 46).

It is to be noticed that Cynics of the stamp of Bion and Teles do not advise any man to renounce riches or pleasure, if they spontaneously come his way. The game with Fortune is properly played if you take every bit of enjoyment that Fortune offers you, but never let yourself become so dependent upon her, that you mind if Fortune takes anything away. "You," Teles says to a rich man, "give liberally and I take valiantly from you, neither grovelling nor demeaning myself basely n or grumbling" (p. 3). One short sermon which states this theory of life one may translate as it stands.

"Fortune is like a playwright who designs a number of parts — the shipwrecked man, the poor man, the exile, the king, the beggar. What the good man has to do is to play well any part with which Fortune may invest him. You have been shipwrecked; very well, give a fine rendering of the part 'Shipwrecked man.' You were rich and have become poor. Play the part 'Poor man' as it ought to be played.

> Be your office great or small,
> Equally at home in all —

contented with whatever clothing, whatever fare, whatever service falls to your lot, like Laertes in Homer:

> With an aged woman to tend him, to set before
> him still
> Meat and drink.

And he slept, as we know, upon a bed of leaves.

"Such a life lacks nothing in pleasantness or healthfulness, so long as one's heart is not set on luxury.

> Not in the belly's glut
> Doth true good stand. (EURIPIDES.)

No, nor in the style of a garment nor in the soft ness of a bed. Euripides says rather happily :
Being luxurious We hunt for new devices of strange foods.

Not foods only, but things to gratify our noses, things to gratify our ears. Our rule should be 'No luxury unless circumstances put it easily in our reach.' We should be like the sailors who observe wind and weather. Is the wind there, use it: no wind, then stop. Or like soldiers again; the man who has a horse serves as a trooper, the man who has heavy armour, serves as a hoplite, the man who has no armour, serves as a psilast, and just as in that case, suppose the enemy make your position uncomfortable by his archery, you fall back, if you are a light-armed soldier, to the protection of the heavy troops, so if at any time you are assailed by war, by poverty, by sickness, retire to the lonely crust, re tire to being your own servant, retire to the poor man's cloak, in the last resort, retire out of the world altogether."

In Lucian's little dialogue entitled *Cynicus* we have a defence of the Cynic way of life put into the mouth of one who practises it. "I have no desire," we find him say, "to be like the men of modern fashion, even if they suppose themselves to have made such a wonderful advance in happiness beyond their ancestors, in the way they eat and the way they dress, sleeking their skins and shaving the hair off their bodies. I boast that my feet are just like the hoofs of horses. I need an artificial bed no more than the lion does. I need expensive food no more than a dog does. Be it mine to have the whole earth for my bed, the whole world for my house, and the food which comes readiest to hand for my fare. Is my appearance not that most seemly for a good man — to be unwashed, to be hairy, to wear a poor man's cloak, to walk bare-foot?... This cloak of mine, which you mock at, this long hair, this appearance of mine, has such power that it enables me to live in peace of mind, to do what I will, to consort with whom I will. For my appearance frightens off all who are fools and uninstructed; soft-livers give me a wide enough berth; but the men of finest temper, the men most truly reasonable, those who hunger after virtue, seek my companionship."

The Cynic sect, as was said just now, went farther than any other in a practical repudiation of the values which governed the ordinary man's life. But the Stoics, as is well known, took over from the outset a great deal of the Cynic teaching and the Cynic ideal. Diogenes was, with Herakles and Socrates, one of the stock typical heroes of later Stoic philosophers. It is not therefore surprising that much in Seneca and Epictetus should be closely parallel to what we read in the sermons of Teles. The figure, for instance, of the actor who has to play well the part assigned him, which recurs in Teles, was also a favourite one with Epictetus.

"Do you not see that Polus did not act Oedipus the king in better voice or with greater pleasure than he acted Oedipus the poor beggar at Colonus? What! is the good man and true to shew himself inferior to Polus, instead of playing any part well that Providence puts upon him? Will he not rather make Odysseus his pattern, who was just as remark able in his rags as in his rich cloak of purple?" [Fragment II. Translation by P. E. Matheson, 1916.]

What is more noteworthy, for our present purpose, than the resemblance between the Cynic and the Stoic is the resemblance between much in the Cynic-Stoic teaching and what we find in the schools regarded as the precise opposite, the schools which made the chief good consist in pleasure. Teles himself on occasion reinforces his sermons by sayings of Aristippus, the founder of the Cyrenaic school. Teles indeed represents a brand of Cynicism which had probably become more assimilated to Aristippus than the founders of Cynicism, Antisthenes and Diogenes, would have approved. In his repeated counsel to use the opportunities for enjoyment when they are there, Teles is more Cyrenaic than true Cynic. When he says to the rich man "I take valiantly what you give" Teles reproduces precisely the position of Aristippus, who maintained that it was no shame that he should enjoy heartily the pleasures which the gifts of kings and tyrants put at his command. But this blending of Cynicism and Cyrenaicism was possible only because there was an element of asceticism in the Cyrenaic philosophy which might seem at first sight incompatible with a philosophy of pleasure. Aristippus too was out to procure αὐτάρκεια, independence of the caprices of Fortune, and he thought he found this independence just as Teles finds it, in keeping your inner detachment all the time you enjoy the gifts of Fortune, so that you are not in the least thrown out, when Fortune withdraws her favours. You score off Fortune, as it were, by taking everything that she offers and never letting your heart get entangled. The Cyrenaic way of deliverance, like that of the other schools, consists in the reduction of interest to a certain narrowly limited field a cutting off of the interests which entangle the heart in things outside this field. The one thing we really possess, said the Cyrenaics, was the present moment. If therefore you savour to the full every bit of enjoyment that the present moment offers, and cut off the interests which make you regret the past, or fear the future, you attain deliverance. So far as it meant this cutting off of interests, there was an ascetic element in the Cyrenaic philosophy. And Aristippus on occasion could show just the same inner detachment which might have been shown in similar circumstances by a Cynic or Stoic. There was the story to which Horace alludes in one of his Satires, how Aristippus was once making a journey over some bit of the African desert with his slaves carrying bags of gold, and how, when the load seemed too much for them, he ordered them simply to throw the gold away.

The ascetic element is still more strongly pronounce in Epicureanism. Perhaps when I read out passages from Teles just now, someone may have been struck by the very close resemblance between the attitude he describes and that described by the Epicurean poet Horace, in the famous stanzas :

> Fortuna, saevo laeta negotio,
> ludum insolentem ludere pertinax,
> transmutat incertos honores,
> nun c mihi, nunc alii benigna.
> laudo manentem, cum celeres quatit
> pinnas, resigno quae dedit et mea
> virtute me ln volvo probamque
> pauperiem sine dote quaero.

That is not Stoic, nor Epicurean, nor the distinctive philosophy of any one school; that is a bit of the popular philosophy common to all the philosophic schools of later antiquity.

According to Epicurus too, deliverance is found by rigidly cutting down the field of interest to a certain small compass. That compass, it is true, is pleasure, Epicurus differing however from the Cyrenaics in denying that the present moment is our only possession. We possess the past too by the Pleasures of memory, upon which Epicurus laid great stress, and in choosing pleasure we have to take account of the future, considering what kind of pleasure has the greatest promise of durability. But when Epicurus says that the chief good is pleasure, you have to understand in that a negative, as well as a positive, assertion; it means that a large amount of interest going out in all directions without profit ought to be negated and cut off. The scientific interest, to know the truth about the world for the sake of knowing, is a vanity. Epicurus is very strong that we only need to know as much about nature as will secure us from being afraid of any imaginary supernatural power behind the movement of the world. For that purpose it is quite enough to see one way, or a number of different ways, in which meteorological phenomena, for instance, *might* have been produced by physical causation, because that shows the hypothesis of divine agency to be unnecessary; but it is mere waste of time to try to find out which of all possible modes of physical causation does, as a matter of fact, bring them about. He says this over and over again in the Letter to Pythocles. And when he comes to explain what he means by pleasure, you find that the true end is not so much pleasure as the absence of pain. And if you strictly limit yourself to this you can secure it by quite simple means and be practically independent of Fortune. You choose the plainest fare, you choose enjoyment that does not involve any violent emotional disturbance, you mark out this field and cut off the interests which range outside of it; then you are safe. "Let us give thanks to blessed Nature," one of his recorded sayings, "that she made necessary things easy to come by, and things difficult to procure unnecessary." For the happiest life a fare of barley-bread and nuts suffices. If he had barley-bread and water, Epicurus said, he was prepared to set his happiness against that of Zeus. He seems to have practised and re commended regular fasting on certain days every month, in order to procure greater independence in the matter of food.

Epicurus was sometimes represented as profligate because certain *hetairai* were amongst his associates. But, as a matter of fact, he seems to have looked rather with dislike upon the emotions of physical love, because of their disturbing character. Thus Lucretius in dwelling upon the discomfort and ugliness of sexual gratification, and Tennyson in his description of the disgust and self-loathing created in Lucretius by the love-potion, seem to have been quite in accord with the feeling of the Master himself.

There is certainly an acetic element here and we can understand why Seneca so continually quotes sayings of Epicurus, as admirable from the Stoic t point of view.

"If you wish to make Pythocles rich, do not add to his money, but subtract from his desires." (*Ep.* 21, 7.)

"I have never wished to please the multitude, because the things which I know the multitude disapproves of, and of the things of which the multitude approves I know nothing." (Ep. 29, IO.)

"You should make yourself the servant of philosophy, so that there may come to you true liberty." (Ep. 8, 7.)

"Poverty brought within the compass of the law of nature is great riches." (Ep. 4, 10.)

"Cheerful poverty is a thing of beauty." (*Ep.* 2, 6.)

"He enjoys riches most, who has least need of riches." (*Ep.* 14, 17.)

"It is especially when you are compelled to be in a crowd that you should retire into yourself." (*Ep.* 25, 6.)

"If what a man possesses does not seem sufficient to him, he will be miserable, even if he becomes lord of the universe." (*Ep.* 9, 20.)

"Excessive anger begets insanity." (*Ep.* 6, 4.)

"The unwise life is disagreeable and full of trouble; it is all reaching out into the future." (*Ep.* 15, 9.)

"The wise man, though he is being roasted in the brazen bull of Phalaris, will exclaim 'O the pleasure that I enjoy! All this is nothing to me." (*Ep.* 66, 18.)

All sects alike, we have seen, aimed at making the individual independent of the play of Fortune, and all sects alike declared that such independence was to be secured by cutting off interests outside a certain prescribed field. They differed when they came to state what the prescribed field was to be. It is plain that supposing you could cut off interest altogether, you would secure complete independence; Fortune would no longer have any purchase at all. The

Cynics went farther than other sects in negating generally recognized values. They abolished, for instance, as we have seen, the interest in cleanliness. Even the Stoics did not do this. Epictetus especially required his disciples to be dressed indeed with extreme plainness, but to be clean and sweet in person. Yet it is plain that if you have an interest in being clean, you are to that extent within the grasp of Fortune; you are certainly more independent if it makes no sort of difference to you whether you are clean or dirty. In the ideal of heroic virtue which came up with Christian monasticism the indifference to cleanliness was, as is well known, a prominent characteristic. Augustine writes in a letter of counsel to some nuns: "Lavacrum etiam corporum ususque balnearum non sit assiduus, sed eo quo solet intervallo temporis tribuatur, hoc est semel in mense."

St Jerome, describing his condition when he was living as a hermit in the Syrian wilderness, writes: "Horrebant sacco membra deformia, et squalida cutis situm aethiopicae carnis obduxerat." "My skin was covered with a coating of dirt which made it look like a negro's."

Christianity was here perfectly in agreement with the Cynic ideal of independence. The Emperor Julian, the would-be champion of Hellenism against Christianity, was wont, Gibbon tells us, to jest about the populousness of his beard.

A thorough cutting off of all interests must no doubt include the interest in cleanliness amongst the rest, and a thorough cutting off of all interests would unquestionably destroy everything by which Fortune has a hold. Why was it that the ancient philosophies could not simply prescribe this thoroughgoing method? Why must they still on? The reason is, of course, that they needed, not only to secure a man independence, but to leave him still some motive for action, and without interest in something no motive for action is possible. If man had been a purely passive being, it might have been possible to advise an extinction of all interest. Because man was under the necessity of acting in some way or other, they were bound to leave him some interest by which action might be prompted and guided. But how can you I give man an interest for action and not, to that extent, sacrifice his independence? This was the standing crux, the essential problem, of the later Greek schools of philosophy. Having cut a man off from the world, as far as you can, for the sake of independence, you had to bring him back to the world as an agent. How was this to be achieved? Epicurus thought you could manage it by cutting down the field of interest to such simple pleasures as you might be pretty sure of having at your command, whatever turn Fortune took. Interest in these would be enough to give the wise man all the motives for action he required, and at the same time not put him dangerously at Fortune's mercy. The Sceptic plan was to bid the man take, as his guide for action, the ordinary conventions of society, which he found established, but to keep his interest in check by telling himself all the time that he did not know whether any object of action was good or evil. The Stoic plan was the most subtle and elaborate. Interest was to be concentrated upon the action itself, never upon the result of the action. A man should have full satisfaction in the consciousness that his action was right, whether the thing he tried to do was achieved or not. But, since action is at any rate directed upon outside things, that leaves one still in need of some principle by which right objects of action may be distinguished from wrong. And so the Stoics planned a scheme of values in outside things — they actually used the word ἀξία — which yet were to be wholly separate from interest — a difficult business, but it seems to me that a figure I once used in a book of mine may help us to understand what they had in their minds. If a servant is sent to fetch a parcel from the post office, his whole action will be determined by the intention to get the parcel, but he will have no interest in the parcel which will make him disappointed if he finds, when he reaches the post office, that the parcel has not arrived. He will be satisfied with having performed the action commanded. Just so, for the Stoic, riches, for instance, are one of the things that have value. If a Stoic is in business he will conduct his transactions in the way which he thinks will course, with be most profitable — consistently, honesty; Reason, God, Nature — of he used all words to mean the same thing commands him in certain circumstances to make the acquisition of wealth the object of his action. But he will be perfectly indifferent as to whether he succeeds. He will do his level best to grow rich, but if, by some caprice of Fortune, his ships are swallowed up by the Icarian Sea under the buffeting of Africus, and he becomes bankrupt, he will not suffer a pang.

That was the object of all the schools, to create in the midst of this rushing, fevered, tumultuous, distracted world the Wise Man, a figure of abiding and unearthly calm. He looks at you with eyes in which there is a benign and radiant serenity — something really unearthly and strangely quelling — because in him the interests by which you and I are driven hither and thither are dead. "Nil admirari prope res est una, Numici, Solaque quae possit facere et servare beatum," says Horace. "Nil admirari" — to be beyond fear and beyond wonder at the spectacle of all this vast world moving round us

> hunc solem et stellas et decedentia certis
> tempora momen tis.

Where men have made this detachment the ideal after which they strive some have really come by self-discipline sufficiently near it to be extraordinarily impressive. In India to-day, where an ideal analogous to the Stoic has prevailed, there are a certain number of individuals who do disconcert Europeans by their appearance of having attained an uncanny satisfaction and tranquillity. There must have been similar figures in the Greco-Roman world. Even Lucian, who mocks so habitually at the false philosophers, occasionally draws the portrait of a true one — Nigrinus, Demonax.

It is certainly impressive, the attainment, or apparent attainment, of this ideal. Yet one must question whether it is one which the human spirit, in its full development, can find adequate. A different ideal was before the minds of the Greeks in the great stirring days of the free city state; a different ideal has been before the modern European world. That other ideal too, so far as it is attained, frees a man from dependence upon Fortune, but it does not free him by cutting off his interest from outside things. On the contrary, his interest is heightened and intensified. Interest, it is felt, is life, and, when all is said and done, the quietness attained in the Stoic, and in the Indian, way, is too like the quietness of death. The alternative ideal is, I think, expresses in the word "a cause." I do not, of course, mean cause as the correlative of effect, but cause in the sense in which we speak of some cause for which men will live and die — a national cause, a religious cause. There seem to me to be three essential elements in the idea of a cause. (I) It is the interest, not of an individual only, but of a great organic body, a society, a community, to which the individual belongs or attaches itself. (2) It implies an effort, extending through time, perhaps through an indefinite number of generations, to realize the common ideal in the outside world of fact. There is a fighting quality in it, a determination to overcome obstacles, to remake the world according to the heart's desire. (3) It implies, as a rule, an optimistic hope, a belief that the victory of the cause may really sooner or later be won. We hear, of course, of people who fight heroically for causes which they know to be irretrievably lost; but it may, I think, be questioned whether anyone fights for a cause for which he has no hope at all; there is probably in the cases spoken of a kind of wild hope that after all, by some unlooked-for chance, one chance in a hundred, the victory may yet be won, and it is that faint chance which makes it worth while to go on fighting.

The citizens of the old free Greek states, the citizens of the Roman Republic, found their happiness, not in detachment, but in the cause of their civic community, by losing themselves as individuals in the great communal passion for promoting the glory and power of Athens or Sparta or Rome. And if one described in a single phrase why.it is that the Hellenistic and Roman world, after political liberty is gone, seems to us, for all the culture, all the economic activity, all the virtue it still embodies, to be steeped in a kind of dead atmosphere, an *aura morta*, we may say that it is a world without causes. There were no great modifications of terrestrial things which were to be brought about by the corporate effort of some society to which this or that man belonged. All that the virtuous man could do was to do his individual duty, to play his part, in a world which was never going to be any better than it was in his own day, nor indeed ever very different, till it broke up in some cosmic cataclysm. We are often told that the decadent Greco-Roman world shows strange analogies to the world to-day, and so it does — the sophistication of life, the craving for sensation, the credulous attraction to the occult. The inference is sometimes made that our own civilization too must be in its dying phase. But the analogies should not make us overlook the enormous difference between those times and our own. Modern times are times in which there is a notable plenitude of causes. There is hardly anyone who is not attached to some cause in whose advance he believes. There are all the national causes: in England there are still people for whom devotion to the old country provides the cause which seems to them to be the one of substantial reality; they look forward to an increase of England's, or of the British Commonwealth's, power and dignity in the world. There are other people for whom the worthiest cause seems to be to establish international co-operation in the place of national antagonisms, for whom the League of Nations, or some League of Nations, seems the thing supremely worth working for. There are others whose cause is the coming of some better political and economic order all over the world — some form of Socialism or Communism. There are others whose cause is more distinctly religious — the coming of the kingdom of God. And we must not forget that notable band of men for whom the increase of scientific knowledge is the great cause, those who watch the gradual victorious advance in different lines of research — one new bit of knowledge to-day, another to-morrow, added to the slowly growing total, and whose lives will seem to them well spent, if one little solid addition is made to that total by their own individual work. The idea of some cause going forward, some cause to which we can contribute, is so bred in the bone of modern men that we can hardly imagine a world in which the hope of improvement and advance is absent.

It would not be true to say that the ideal of emancipation in the ancient world was entirely individualistic and selfish. No people have laid greater stress than the Stoics did, for instance, upon the individual's solidarity with the Universe, and especially with other rational beings. Epictetus, Seneca, Marcus Aurelius, are full of the duty incumbent upon the individual to serve and help his fellow-men; we are none of us, they continually say, born for ourselves alone. That may seem to come near to what I described as a cause, and it certainly has one element of a cause, the recognition by the individual of a larger body to which he belongs and whose interests he is bound to make his own. But it seems to me to lack the other elements in a cause — the conception of some particular end to be realized by corporate effort in the actual world and the hope of that end being achieved. According to the Stoic idea, the good man has simply to play his part nobly in a world which is never going to be very different. That is the still, sad note of Marcus Aurelius. The phrase "play his part" gives indeed the figure to which, as we have seen, the practical philosophy of the Hellenistic age habitually recurs — the figure of the actor in a play. And that is significant. The actor, unlike the soldier, is not helping by his effort to decide an issue still undetermined, he is not engaged in any struggle for a cause, he is just going through, well or ill, the fixed part assigned.

Perhaps I should try to explain what I meant just now when I said that devotion to a cause, whilst it directed interest upon outside things, nevertheless made a man independent of Fortune. For it is quite obvious that the advance or setting back of a cause does depend, like the prosperity of an individual, upon many outside accidents; causes upon which men have set their hearts sometimes come to grief and finally fail. But the point is this: because the interest embodied in the cause is the interest of a community and because the life of a community reach es out into an unknown future beyond the life of the individual, a set-back to the cause in which a man is interested may leave his hope of its ultimate triumph unshaken. His hope may in the end prove to have been a delusion, but it can hardly ever be proved to the man himself that it is a delusion. The utmost malice of Fortune may leave him still confident; he may fall himself in fighting for the cause and die happy,because his interest has ceased, as the psychologists say, to be egocentric and has been transferred to the being of the beloved community. "Who dies, if England lives?" The vitality of some causes in the face of what would seem overwhelming facts is astounding. One would say, for instance, that if any cause definitively and for ever failed, the national cause for which the Mexicans under Montezuma fought against the incoming Spaniards 400 years ago did so. I was told however not long ago by someone who knew intimately the native peoples of New Mexico that they cherished still, by a secret tradition, the unconquerable belief that Montezuma was not really dead, that one day he would come back and drive out the white man and restore the world as it was before. In some villages it was the custom for a man to climb every day before daybreak to the top of a neighbouring hill and all alone watch the dawn, because that might be the day when Montezuma would return. A man who has lost himself in a great cause is, if not invulnerable by Fortune, at any rate safe from utter overthrow.

Into the dead atmosphere of the Greco-Roman world came Christianity. The question has often been asked what Christianity brought that world which it had not got already. To a large extent the ethics of the Christian Church and the ethics of the Hellenistic moralists ran together. It is claimed sometimes that the theological beliefs and ritual practices of the Church had their close Hellenistic parallels. What then, it is asked,was there special and distinctive about Christianity? No doubt many answers may be properly given to that question, but there is one short answer which I think will serve. I was a cause. That is why it came into the dead atmosphere like a breath of new air. Men drawn into this society felt that they came into a stream of more than individual life, setting through time towards a great victory. The life of this community was indestructible; the will embodied in it was a Divine Will by which all outside things were to be ultimately shaped and subdued; men I might be fellow-workers with God towards the great end; they might give the cause the supreme sacrifice of their lives.

No doubt this distinctive note of Christianity was due to its Hebraic origin, as distinguished from those elements of Hellenism which it absorbed. It carried on the hope of ancient Israel a communal hope, an expectation of the Day of Israel's God. Christianity has remained always essentially Hebraic. We hear a great deal to-day about Saint Paul and the Hellenistic mystery-religions. Striking parallels have been pointed out: in the Greek mystic sects too a man received apparently a new supernatural life through some initiation, and there were ceremonial rites of admission and of membership, which show analogy to baptism and the eucharist. Some people have been therefore disposed to regard Christianity, in the form given it by Saint Paul, as simply one more mystery-religion added to the rest. But this is to overlook the most esential thing in Christianity — that which constituted it a cause. In the Hellenistic mystery-religions the man who received initiation was simply lifted out of the lower sphere, individually, into the higher sphere; there was, so far as we know, no common purpose which the society was set to achieve in the real world. The man brought into the Christian community was brought into a stream of dynamic life going through time towards a definite consummation, a divine event, in the future. That remained essential to Christianity, even when it later on borrowed Hellenistic moulds in which to cast its dogmas: we must not be misled by the Greek modes of thought and expression so as to overlook the abiding Hebrew core — the ruling idea that here was a Divine Society called to work and fight through the ages towards a consummation on beyond, even if delayed, none the less sure. You get it put in the forefront by Saint Augustine in his idea of the Civitas Dei, the Society which he sees running through human history, from the first beginning of man, contending in each age under varying tribulations, for the one great cause, with the assurance of ultimate triumph.

To-day,as I have said, we have such a plenitude of causes inviting our devotion, that it is difficult perhaps to realize what the teaching of the old philosophies meant for those to whom the movement of the world was an unrest leading nowhere. To day we may question the belief in progress as an abstract proposition, but it is so inwoven in our thoughts that it is difficult for us to divest ourselves of it. The actual fact of progress in certain lines is too near to us and too obvious — the astonishing advances which science has made in recent times and is still making, the raising of the standard of life, at any rate on the side of material comfort, for those who do the manual work of our civilization, the growing possibilities of human intercourse which are unifying the globe to a degree unknown ever before. But supposing we were ever in our Western world to lose this assurance of progress, recent as it indeed is, supposing we were to become thoroughly disillusioned by future adverse experience, as to any national cause being worth fighting for, as to any international harmony being practicable, as to any new social order removing present evils, as to the advance of science continuing, or, if it did continue, increasing human happiness, and supposing at the same time men lost the supernatural hope which makes Christi anity, as George Tyrrell said in his last pathetic book, if a pessimism so far as this earth goes, yet an optimism with regard to the sum of things — supposing this happened, then, I fancy, the best men would once more feel that in such a world there was nothing for them to do except just to realize in their own individual lives an ideal of dignity — to play their part creditably. To them the allusion with which Teles closes one of his sermons, and which Cicero and Seneca and others repeat after him, would come home: "That was a fine gesture of the skipper's: 'You may sink her, Poseidon, but true to her course it is that she'll go down.' So may a good man say to Fortune: 'But it is a man that you'll find, no shirker, no coward.'"

The Social Question in the Third Century

I AM going to speak this afternoon about one aspect of the social problems of the century after Alexander, the conditions that made for social revolution. I shall start from an extraordinary provision in a mortgage deed, which only seems explicable from the social background of the time; and we shall have to see what that background was, which means wealth and poverty, and consider the great economic disturbance in the generation after Alexander, and how it affected the working man, which means prices and wages. Thanks to the temple accounts at Delos, though at present they are only published completely from 314 to 250, we have now something definite to go on; and we can compare them with various fourth century accounts, especially those of Eleusis in 329. We shall see that the gulf between rich and poor has become wider, and that underneath the brilliant civilization of the third century lies the fear of social revolution. Finally I shall say something, from the social side, about the revolution at Sparta, as it is our best account of a social revolution.

The mortgage in question dates from early in the third century, when many of the Islands were borrowing to pay Demetrius' taxes. Praxicles of Naxos lends three talents to the city of Arcesine in Amorgos at 10% interest, and the city mortgages to him all its own property, all its citizen's property, and all its metics' property, both in Amorgos or overseas; and it is provided that the city shall not pass any law or do anything which shall override the mortgage. The other provisions I need not go into now. The usual explanation of this deed has been that the islands were very poor (we shall see that that was not the case) and that Arcesine's credit must have been utterly ruined for the city to con sent to such terms. Unfortunately, Arcesine's credit was particularly good, as one can see from the rate of interest on another loan. In the fourth century the usual rate on mortgages and loans other than mercantile loans had been 12%, except for the temple at Delos, which lent at 10% throughout its history; but 12% could not survive cheap money, and the last cases of it we meet are at Teos about 300 and at Arcesine soon after. Praxicles' mortgage seems to be the first case, outside Delos, of 10% which became the usual rate in the third century, and is found at Ilium, at Oropus, and at Peraea. But Arcesine raised a third loan about this time at $8\frac{1}{3}$%, the lowest business rate known for nearly a century; for the 6% which occurs in a loan to Miletus in 282 seems to be a favour, into which political reasons enter. This loan at $8\frac{1}{3}$% shows that Arcesine was really pretty prosperous; one may also notice that the city had no need to entice anyone to lend it money by promising honours to the lender, as some cities did in the second century. Yet, in spite of this, does not the city give Praxicles an absurd amount of security for the small sum of three talents? A city generally mortgaged either certain lands or certain revenues, as for instance Delos always mortgaged its 2% import and export duties; but extraordinary mortgages do occur, as when Lampsacus in the fourth century mortgaged its Acropolis, and perhaps it does not really mean much for a small city to mortgage all its property, provided it meant to pay. Similarly, a mortgage of the property of all the citizens is only an extension, though a considerable extension, of the usual practice, which was to mortgage the property of *certain* citizens as sureties; Miletus in 282 thus mortgages the property of no less than 75 citizens. But what *is* extraordinary is to mortgage the property of metics; and the fact that we know of one or two- other cases of this in the third century does not make it less so. Metics of course were still looked down upon, as Teles shows, and Heraclides frankly calls their position at Athens one of servitude; while the wood and charcoal law at Delos was soon going to revive the bad old custom of allowing a creditor to seize the metic's person. Still, even so, as Praxicles' security was ample, *why* was metics' property inserted? The answer is to be found in the inclusion of overseas property, which here means ships and their cargoes, as Arcesine owned no property overseas. For metics were often traders and ship-owners; and the right given to Praxicles to seize metics' property as well as citizens' property really means the right to seize any ship belonging to any inhabitant of Arcesin e without enquiring as to the owner's status. If he insisted on this right, he must have thought that his security over property in Arcesine itself might become valueless; and only one thing could make it valueless, a revolution and cancellation of debts. In that case he could get nothing from the city; but he could still seize a ship, and there are two cases known where mortgagees did seize ships. That is why he inserted the clause forbidding the city to pass any law overriding the mortgage. Naturally it could not be enforced; a city could pass any law it pleased, and there had recently been a famous case at Ephesus, where mortgages on land had become so heavy that the government had constituted itself a committee of public safety and compelled all mortgagees to accept what was in effect part payment only. But the clause meant that, if a revolutionary government cancelled Praxicles' mortgage, and he seized a ship, and the matter came to negotiation or arbitration, as it probably would, he could fairly claim that he was within his legal rights. I may add that there was nothing in all this to hurt Arcesine in the least, provided she meant to pay. It used to be suggested that her credit *must* have been very bad or she could have borrowed from the temple at Delos on simpler terms. But this depended, not on her credit, which was good enough,but on the temple. The temple at this time had only eight or nine talents of liquid funds available for lending; the city of Delos had first call on this, and one fair-sized loan, like the five talents lent to Hermione in 274, would exhaust the balance; it was just a chance at any moment whether Apollo *could* lend you three talents. Besides, if you borrowed from a private person you could, if you chose, procrastinate a good deal over payment — there are some extraordinary cases; but Apollo could appeal to his suzerain, and you might get a visit from that suzerain's fleet; that did happen.

Now why was Praxicles, in the prosperous world in which he lived,afraid of revolution? For the century after Alexander *was* a prosperous time for the upper classes in most places; Polybius' lamentations about the state of Greece belong to a much later period. I suppose now one need hardly enlarge on this prosperity. One sees it in things like the great number of new festivals which appear and the growth of a class of professional actors and athletes for their service; in the outburst of new associations round about 300, and in particular of social clubs, *eranoi*, where the subscriptions were of importance; in the growth of table luxury; above all, in the expansion of trade, of which I may give one very simple illustration: about 400 the annual produce of the 2% import and export duties at Athens was round about 200,000 drachmae; at Rhodes, which had taken Athens' place, it had by 170 reached a million. But as at present we are talking about the island world, I will give some definite indications of that prosperity in the islands, taking Rhodes and Delos for granted. Th e only business rates of interest lower than the standard 10% which we meet in the third century are in the islands; $8\frac{1}{3}$% at Arcesine, and at the end of the century 7% as the normal rate in Thera. That is, capital was cheap. We possess from Mykonos part of a register of dowries, eight entries. The two highest are 14,000 and I0,000 drachmae, that is, they average two talents. I think we only know one certain case of a dowry of as much as two talents in fourth century Athens, and two or three of one talent. On the other hand, a list has been published of Athenian dowries collected from the inscriptions, fourth to second centuries, eleven in all; the average of these Athenian dowries is 2840 drachmae, that of the Mykonos dowries is 4450. We possess from Tenos part of a register of sales of real property, third century. The entries are very numerous indeed, and bear witness to a flourishing commercial community in which there was a ready market for land. In some cases the vendor allows the whole of the purchase-money to remain on mortgage; very optimistic, but it does show confidence in the future of real property in the island. About 200 the island of Cos raised a voluntary subscription to equip a fleet. Two hundred and twenty subscriptions are extant; they include one of 7000 dr., one of 4000, seven of 3000, and twenty-two of 1,000 and over. I think this is a higher level than we meet anywhere except perhaps in Demosthenes' Athens; the largest subscription is identical with the largest subscription given toward the new temple at Delphi in the fourth century, and that was given by Sparta, then the richest state in Greece. The prosperity of Cos is confirmed by the great number of religious embassies sent from Cos to Delos in the third century, one of which was conducted by Theocritus' friend, the Aratus of the sixth and seventh idyls, who can now be identified in the inscriptions. There is also the evidence of the clubs. In Epicteta's association at Thera the fines for breach of the rules ran from 150 to 500 drachmae, while the highest fine in any association at Athens was 50 drachmae; and it was in the islands, at Cos and Thera, that the third century clubs started the practice, when they honoured members, of substituting a gold crown for one of green leaves. I may add that two islands, Thera and Siphnos, both honour Egyptian officials with crowns of 2000 drachmae, which is enormous as crowns went; I think you never get over 1,000 drachmae at Athens. These sort of items do indicate a good deal of prosperity among the upper classes. It is no objection to this that various islands borrowed money to pay Demetrius' taxes. For one thing, they had borrowed much more heavily during the second Athenian confederacy; and for another,borrowing is no sign of poverty in a city — London, for example. It seems certain that some Greek cities in the third century *did* understand systematic borrowing; Delos for instance was regularly financed by the temple, as some modern businesses are by their bankers; the city was constantly borrowing and repaying, and sometimes it repaid very quickly; thus in 282 it borrowed 25,000 drachmae and repaid nearly 20,000 the same year. A Greek city had no budget and as a rule no reserve; it merely earmarked certain receipts to certain expenses; if a new expense arose, like a war contribution, it had to levy a special tax, or raise a subscription, which took time; it was a *convenience* to borrow the amount and then pay off the debt at leisure, and that is all that much of the borrowing comes to. To give one simple illustration. In 180, Delos had a large sum on deposit in the temple, and yet borrowed 100 dr. from the temple for a crown for somebody; the reason was that the money on deposit belonged to an account which was earmarked for the city's corn supply.

The third century then was a prosperous time for the upper classes, just as one would expect from the brilliant culture of the period. But when we turn to the lower classes, we shall find conditions exactly reversed; they were definitely worse off than they had been; speaking generally, prices were up and wages were down. The first thing to look at is the economic disturbance caused by Alexander's release of the Persian treasure, a disturbance which followed right upon the very considerable rise in prices which had taken place in the two generations before Alexander, caused by the secularization of the temple treasures at Athens, Delphi, and elsewhere. Let me remind you what the Persian treasure meant. Athens began the Peloponnesian War with 6000 talents in hand. Apollo of Delphi, before the Sacred War, was traditionally worth 10,000 talents. Alexander secured 180,000 talents in coined money, and perhaps an equal amount in bullion, plate, and so on. Naturally the economic disturbance in Greece was very great. One ought to be able to show it by price curves. Unfortunately the curve I should like to give, wheat, is not complete enough; and one complete curve,the price of pitch, is useless for my purpose; for pitch was a monopoly, and political reasons enter into the price. I have however taken out two curves which I think are new and are free from objection; one is the wages of a hoplite — citizen troops, not mercenaries — and the other is the rent of the farms belonging to the temple at Delos. In the Peloponnesian War a hoplite got a drachma a day at Athens, but not much over four obols, Athenian currency, in the Peloponnese. (I am including in wages the so called food allowance, which often is not distinguished.) At the beginning of Alexander's reign the hoplites of the states in the League of Corinth probably all got a drachma a day, as that was what Alexander paid his best heavy infantry, the hypaspists; anyhow, they cannot have got more. But in 303, when Demetrius re-formed the League of Corinth, the hoplites of the League states were getting two drachmae a day, just double. In the treaty between Aetolia and Acarnania of about 272 they still get two drachmae, but they are Corinthian drachmae, say eight obols in Athenian currency; soon after 229 Antigonus Doson is paying about the same; and about 200 Rhodes is paying nine Rhodian obols, which is again about eight obols in Athenian currency. That is, between 335 and 303 a hoplite's pay doubled; in the third century it fell back again, but still remained 33% higher than the old standard. Now the farm rents. I take only the 15 farms which the temple had always possessed, and omit the farms purchased at the beginning of the third century. The total rent of those 15 farms in drachmae, omitting sums under 100, is as follows. In 434 it was from about 7500 to 7600. In the four years 377 to 374 it was 7800. At the letting of 314, the first year of Delos' freedom, it was 11,500, an enormous rise. In 305 it was 14,300; at the letting of 300 it was 16,200, the highest point touched. In 290 it is only 9600, an exaggerated fall which must be due partly to external reasons, perhaps the threatened descent of Etruscan pirates; for in 280 it recovers to 10,300 and in 270 to 11,300, and here I imagine we are on the true curve again. In 260 it has fallen to 8800, and here the real rise in the value of money shows itself. In 250 there is a slight recovery to 9300; but by 220 it is down to 6100, and by 179 to 5900. That is, in 300 the rents are more than double the highest figure of the period before Alexander. Taken together, these two curves justify us in supposing that the lowest value of money, that is, the highest prices, were round about 300, and that the drachma at that time was not worth more than 50%, or say three obols. One can confirm this by the fact that at Demetrius' siege of Rhodes in 304 the ransom fixed for a free captive was 1000 drachmae, as against 300 to 500 in the Sacred War. The culminating point cannot have been much earlier than about 300; for the law which regulated the letting of the farms at Delos, passed a year or two before 300, provided that a tenant could hold on for a second term, with out having to bid at the auction, on paying 10% increase of rent; that is, money was falling in value.

I come now to the main question, how did all this affect the working classes? Here we must turn to Delos. First, their expenditure — that is the price of food, clothing, housing, and fuel. I may leave out fuel, for the price of firewood at Delos down to 258, when there was a temporary fall, remained much the same as at Eleusis in 329. Clothes also seem to vary very little, though our information is too meagre to argue from. But the rise in the cost of food and housing was great. I take food first; and the most important food to the working man was corn. Now at Delos barley was normally about half the price of wheat, and a man when paid in kind was given indifferently either so much wheat or double the amount of barley, so I may calculate in wheat only. Demosthenes says that prior to the famine of 329 the normal or regular price of wheat at Athens was five drachmae the bushel, which may serve as a base-line; for both Athens and Delos imported wheat by sea. Taking the year's average, in 282 wheat at Delos was 7 dr. 3 obols the bushel (it touched 10 drachmae); in 258 it was 6 dr. 4 obols; in 250 it was 5 dr. 4 obols. We have no figures round about 300; but as the farm rents *must* bear *some* relation to the price of wheat, then, looking at the money curve, I should expect wheat about 300 to average ten drachmae; and it was possibly about this time that barley at Lampsacus was 6 drachmae, which would be 10 to 12 drachmae for wheat. However, we see that by 250 wheat had not yet got back to the basic figure, any more than farm rents had; and in fact, more than half a century later the established official price at Samos was still somewhat over the ' basic figure, 5 dr. 2 obols. But if the working man was badly off with the price of wheat, he was still worse off for oil, one of the few absolute necessities of the very poorest, as Menander says, for they had no other fats. In the early fourth century oil was 12 drachmae the metretes. At Delos, about 305, it averaged 42 drachmae; in 302 it was 45. By 281 it had fallen to 36, and from 269 to 250 it fluctuates between 20 and 16; that is, like wheat, it had still not got back to the old price.

Common wine was much the same; Demosthenes gives 4 dr. the metretes as the normal price, while at Delos it fluctuates between 10 and $11\frac{1}{2}$. Housing was even worse than food. (After the first quarter of the third century the working population at Delos was fast increasing; so I assume that, if better houses rise in value, poorer ones rose also.) I have taken out the average rent of a house for the houses belonging to the temple (the lettings vary in number, so totals are useless). Early in the fourth century the average annual rent was certainly not over 20 dr. and was probably nearer 10. Unfortunately there are no figures about 300; but in 282 the average is 38, at least double. In 279 it is 61, from which it rises steadily to 73 in 250, that is, four or five times the figure before Alexander. The rents are already going against the general price curve, rising while money is rising, because people had already begun to flock into Delos. In 246 there was a house famine, and the figure jumps to 125; in 219 it is 73 again, and thence rises again to over 100 in the early second century. The point is, that if working men came to Delos for work with housing in that state, what were the general conditions like in the places they came from?

We now come to the important question of wages. Looking at the great rise in the price of food and housing in the first part of the third century, wages ought to have risen considerably. For in the time before Alexander wages *had* done so. Wheat had risen from three drachmae a bushel in Socrates' time to five drachmae in Demosthenes'; but wages had risen even more; at the end of the fifth century a skilled artisan at Athens got a drachma a day, at Delphi about 339 he was getting, in Athenian currency, about $8\frac{1}{3}$ obols, at Eleusis in 329 he generally got $2\frac{1}{2}$ drachmae — 15 obols. But after Alexander we find that the wages at Delos, instead of rising with rising prices, actually fall. We need a base-line for comparison, the level of bare subsistence, and fortunately this is not in doubt; two obols a day for one man, or 120 drachmae the year of 360 days. This was the slave rate, the pauper rate — Menander makes a young man call it a starvation rate; it was what Athens in the late fourth and the third centuries paid to the crippled who could not work, what Delos paid to the temple slaves and the flute-girls, and what Demosthenes had calculated would do for patriotic Athenian troops if they forewent their pay. A man needed one choenix of wheat a day, that is, $7\frac{1}{2}$ bushels (*medimnoi*) a year: and as we know from the Delos accounts that a working-man's *opson* — that is, all food except bread was reckoned at the equivalent in money of his bread, then with wheat at the basic price of five drachmae the man's bare food would cost 75 drachmae a year. We can calculate from the Eleusis and Delos accounts that 15 drachmae a year would do for clothes, if an outfit lasted three years and he had no change of clothing; that leaves the man, out of his 120 drachmae, 30 for housing, fuel, and everything else; that is, two obols a day was just bare existence. For a small family, wife and two children, the line of bare subsistence was probably three times this, a drachma a day or 360 drachmae a year; I may quote a law of Ilium of about 280, whereby a slave, if he murders a tyrant of the city, is to get a drachma a day for life, that is, he shall not have to work for his family. Now to apply these standards — two obols for a man, 1drachma for a family to what we learn about Delos.

First, the daily wage of skilled artisans. At Eleusis in 329 they generally got $2\frac{1}{2}$ drachmae a day. At Delos they practically always get two drachmae. This is a considerable fall; still, on the face of it, two drachmae looks comfortable. The reality was very different. It was two drachmae a day *when employed*, and the employment was merely irregular jobs. (It was no doubt the same at Athens; in one of the broken Erechtheum accounts some named workers seem only to work for a few days in the prytany of 30 days.) I have taken out a few figures for Delos. In 302, a worker called Olympos, who gets more jobs than anyone else, makes not much over 200 drachmae in the year, — let us be liberal and call it 240 — that is, four obols a day, not enough for a family with wheat at five drachmae, and wheat was probably nearer 10. In 279 we have complete figures; I take the most prominent work people. Theodemos the carpenter makes 106 drachmae in the year, not enough to keep himself. Nicon the mason, who had come from Syros to better himself, makes 187 drachmae; he might just maintain a wife. Dexios the black smith only makes $54\frac{1}{2}$ drachmae. A blacksmith would get some work on the farms; but the other two would not get much work apart from the temple. Now this is the real point here — could they get much other work or not? — and so I give the proof that they could not, which is due to Professor Glotz of Paris. In 282 the temple engaged two skilled masons, Leptines and Bacchios, by the year, not by the day, and paid them partly in kind; but by 279, consequent on a temporary famine in 281, when wheat went to 12 drachmae as the year's average, the temple had thrown the risk on the two workmen and had commuted their pay to a money payment totalling altogether 240 drachmae a year each, with an occasional small allowance for clothes — 17 drachmae in 279, nothing in 278. These men would earn two drachmae a day, and 360 days at two drachmae would be 720 drachmae — what the architects got; but these masons are content, for the sake of a permanent engagement by the year, to take exactly one-third of this, 240 drachmae a year or four obols a day — just about what Olympos did make in 302; this shows they could not count on getting outside jobs. The two drachmae a day of the skilled artisan on intermittent jobwork then really means, at best, four obols a day by the year; and this seems to be what Ptolemy III paid to the masons whom he sent to Rhodes after the great earthquake. How did four obols work out for a married man in 279, with wheat at (say) about 7 drachmae? His own food would cost 105 drachmae; his wife's, say two-thirds, 70 drachmae. Suppose he was given his clothes, and his wife's only cost 10 drachmae a year. That leaves 55 drachmae for housing, fuel, and all other expenses, including feeding and clothing his children. That family must have gone very short indeed; still, they had a certainty; they could live somehow or other.

But how did it stand with the great majority who were not engaged by the year? (Remember I am taking the best paid cases.) I will give one illustration, Dexios the blacksmith again. In 281 Dexios and another man undertake to sharpen all the tools of the workmen employed by the temple during the year at one obol apiece. Dexios' half of this is 144 tools at 24 drachmae. In 274 Dexios alone does all the tools at half an obol each; the number has greatly increased, and he does 636 tools for 53 drachmae. That is, in the course of seven years Dexios has come down to doing $4\frac{1}{2}$ times the work for $2\frac{1}{4}$ times the wages. It shows how desperately in need he was of that extra 29 drachmae.

Now to look at the unskilled men. In 329, at Eleusis, they get nine obols a day on jobwork. In 279 at Delos the pay ranges from eight to five obols, but a later fragment shows that one drachma was the normal pay on jobwork, even for the semi-skilled, so I take one drachma as the average, a considerable fall from nine obols to six. But, if two drachmae on job work really meant, as we have seen, only four obols a day by the year, one drachma on the same work was really two obols a day by the year; that is, the bare subsistence line for a single man, the pauper and slave rate. At Delos then one can speak with some confidence on a much controverted question; slave labour *had* dragged unskilled free labour down to its own level. Indeed it sometimes falls lower still, well below the slave rate, though the slave rate it self had fallen; the temple slaves at Eleusis got three obols a day against the two obols at Delos; still even at Delos three obols occurs occasionally, apparently after long service. But I can give two instances of free labour at a rate well below two obols a day per year. In 301, Tlesis, a skilled plasterer, takes on a job for a lump sum of 140 drachmae, which at the usual two drachmae a day means 70 days' work. The temple gives him two labourers to bring sand for him and make and mix his plaster, and pays each of them 30 drachmae for the job, slightly over $2\frac{1}{2}$ obols a day for jobwork instead of a drachma; and wheat may have been 10 drachmae at the time. Those two labourers lived on barley-bread and water, and not too much bread. In 282 the temple employed a woman called Artemisia, not a slave, to do baking, paying her monthly. Her wages for seven months are less than an obol a day; one hopes she was only working for pocket-money. It may be worth mentioning here that the only strike I know of prior to the Roman period was an attempted strike of bakers, at Paros.

We see then that in the first half of the third century the daily wage for both skilled and unskilled labour had fallen considerably since Demothenes' time, though the price of necessities had risen. The same seems true, generally speaking, of piecework. The bulk of the work at Delos, as in all the temple accounts we have, was piecework; but it is too complicated a problem to discuss now, and I can only say that it is supposed to have aggravated the fall in daily wages; certainly some piecework wages fall between 300 and 250. I can however give one set of figures which stands by itself, the cost of cutting the accounts on the actual stones; but I have to omit any Athenian figures, as Athens paid on some totally different system. (For convenience of comparison with Delos I have turned Aeginetan currency into Athenian through out.) Early in the fourth century, at Epidaurus, the tariff per 100 letters cut was usually nine obols; 11 obols and eight obols do both occur, but seem exceptional prices for small pieces of work. At Delphi in 339 the tariff is $8\frac{1}{2}$ obols the 100, but in 335 it has fallen to just under six obols. At Delos in 302 it is still six obols, one drachma, per 100; but later in the year 30 letters are cut for a drachma. In 301 there is a further heavy fall, that is, far more letters are cut for a drachma; and by 282 we find a well-established tariff of 300 letters for a drachma — two obols the 100 — which continues into the second century, and is found then both at Delos and at Lebadea. In 250 an attempt was even made at Delos to get 350 letters cut for a drachma, but it led to bad work, and was apparently given up. Omitting the exceptional extremes, this means that in the course of the century prior to 282 the tariff fell from nine obols to two obols the 100, while most of the time prices were rising and money falling in value. These startling figures more than bear out the deductions I have drawn from the daily wages.

The position of the working man in the third century at Delos was then a very bad one; the unskilled easily fall below the bare level of subsistence, and the skilled are very hard put to it to bring up even one or two children. Yet Delos was a bright spot; by 279 certainly, and probably earlier, work men were going there from other parts of Greece, especially from the islands, which means that their conditions at home were worse. As we have seen something of the property of the upper class in the islands, the deduction is that, so far as the island world can inform us, the third century on the social side was getting into a very unhealthy state; the poor were getting poorer, and the gap between rich and poor was widening. We have seen that from 400 to 329 wages rose with the rise in prices; after Alexander's time wages seem to lose all relation to prices, and fall while prices still rise. The fact seems certain; but I have no explanation to offer beyond unrestrained competition, unless the great wars of the Successors had driven men a little mad. It was not I think Asiatic competition; we do not meet Asiatic workmen at Delos much before 250. But it was competition with little to temper it. There were no workmen's organizations in our sense; associations of men in particular trades are just beginning to appear, but they were only social and religious bodies, which at best might help an oppressed member or give him a decent funeral. Except I think at Athens and Rhodes, state aid was only given during a siege or a famine; and even at Athens it was confined to men definitely crippled. Rhodes later on apparently had a wonderful system of food liturgies, under which wealthy individuals undertook to look after a certain number of poor, perhaps the reason why Rhodes never had any trouble; but it is uncertain when the system started. Philanthropy, in our sense, is a very rare phenomenon; rich men were often liberal, but only to the State. A feeling of humanity was certainly growing, as exhibited in the increase of arbitration, the movement for making whole cities asylums, the habit of manumitting slaves by will, and the dislike of selling free captives; but this had nothing specifically to do with the poor. A copy-book maxim of the time says "Pity slaves"; but as to free men, though we often hear in literature that poverty is hateful — an anonymous fragment of verse says "his own mother hates a poor man" — there seems to be only one doubtful reference to poverty, prior to Cercidas, as a matter for compassion. When the Stoic Cleanthes, in his Hymn to Zeus, says "that which is dear to none other is dear unto thee," he *may* mean the poor and unfortunate; but, even if he does, he leaves the matter to Zeus; he does not suggest that it is any concern of other men.

What we get then is, more *visible* luxury among the rich; high prices and falling wages for the poor; and hardly any shock-absorbers in the social system. These are conditions which lead to trouble; and In fact if things got too bad there was only one known resource, revolution; not political revolution, but social revolution; a rising of the "have-nots" against the "haves," to the cry of division of the land and cancellation of debts. Debt in fact was often at the bottom of the whole business. Praxicles may well have expressed his fear of revolution in his mortgage deed; for troubles between creditors and debtors were common enough in the islands. Between about 280 and 250 we know of at least four outbreaks of the kind in the islands, in Naxos, Amorgos, Ceos, and Syros — one at least is expressly called a matter between poor and rich; and in every case the trouble was bad enough to compel the suzerain power — Egypt or Macedonia — to intervene in order to settle what was probably incipient revolution. But indeed revolution had long been the general fear of the well-to-do; at Athens the jurymen had for centuries taken an oath not to vote for division of land or cancellation of debts; the threat colours many passages in Aristotle; Isocrates had said bluntly that men feared their fellow-citizens more than a foreign enemy. But with the advent of Macedonia, precaution had been substituted for fears. In the treaties made in 335 between Alexander and the States of the League of Corinth it was provided that the Council of the League and Alexander's representative were to see to it that in no city of the League should there be either confiscation of personal property, or division of land, or cancellation of debt, or liberation of slaves for the purpose of revolution. We have here both the complete program me of the social revolution under four heads, and an interstate guarantee against it; if revolution breaks out in any city it is to be repressed by the full force of Macedonia and the Panhellenic League. Demetrius' League of 303, which was a close copy of Alexander's, must have had a similar arrangement; for since 335 conditions had become much worse, and it was probably only the enormous demand for mercenaries, with opportunities of plunder, which tided the Greek world over the economic crisis round about 300. When the social revolution broke out in Cassandreia about 279 this opportunity was already becoming limited; and it was still more limited when in 223 Antigonus Doson of Macedonia formed the third of the Panhellenic Leagues to crush a particular revolution, that at Sparta.

Sparta offers us a picture of the three regular phases of a revolution; drastic reform, moderate or limited revolution, and complete revolution, all within the compass of about one generation. The story is of interest from many sides, personal, military, political, and above all philosophical; but I must confine myself as far as I can to the social aspect. While those writers who were enemies of the movement, Aratus and Polybius, give us much political and military information, it happens that our social information is largely drawn from a convinced friend of the revolution, the contemporary historian Phylarchus, represented for us by Plutarch's Lives of Agis and Cleomenes. Phylarchus was a powerful and dramatic writer, but an out-and-out partisan and untrustworthy over figures; and people once used to doubt his gloomy picture of Sparta in 244, when the young king Agis IV came to the throne. There can however be little question now that that picture is substantially true. He represents the citizen body as enormously reduced, all the land in the hands of a small class of wealthy men, too much property owned by women, and a large number of poor men who had lost their land and consequently, under the Spar tan constitution, their citizenship; the common meals had become a farce, as the rich would not, and the poor could not, take part in them; and both landowners (and poor were weighed down by debts. Now, except for the common meals and the debts, this is exactly the picture Aristotle had drawn nearly a century earlier, only the process had gone a little further. One can trace what had happened. The I Spartan s in Plato's time had been enormously rich in gold and silver, the plunder of war. Since then all their wars at home had been unsuccessful, but against that many Spartan s in the fourth century had made money by military service in Asia and Egypt. There was practically no outlet for money at Sparta itself in commerce or manufactures, so those who owned what remained of all this wealth had invested it in buying up land; this, joined to the loss of Messenia, had rendered a large class landless, and the only wealthy people were the large land owners, unless a few metics. But whereas in the fourth century Sparta had always recovered from defeat, a new thing had happened; she had not recovered from her great defeat by Antigonus Gonatas in 265, for soon afterwards Megalopolis could and did defeat her single-handed; so Phylarch us must be quite right about the enormous reduction in citizens. Then as to debts. Some landowners were still rich in gold, but others were not; there were two classes, as we shall see, and the latter class ad heavily mortgaged their lands in order to live up to the prevailing standard of luxury. One recalls here that, even at Athens, Menander had called a man whose land was not mortgaged very lucky, and that at Ephesus after 297 the heavy mortgages had led to a suspension of the ordinary law; again we have no reason to doubt Phylarchus. As to the poor being burdened with debt, how could anything else possibly happen, looking at the condition of things we saw at Delos? Even at Delos the temple throughout the third century keeps on making an increasing number of bad debts for small amounts, and I have already mentioned the troubles in the islands overdebt; but the best commentary on Phylarchus is Menander's play *The Hero*, where the supposed son and daughter of a poor man go out voluntarily as slaves to work off a debt which is only 200 drachmae. In fact, Menander defines a well-to-do man as "one who can live without borrowing." What we see then at Sparta is what we saw in the islands, only more markedly so; the gulf between rich and poor I has widened; the rich may not be richer, but the poor are much poorer. And as there was practically 1 no middle class at Sparta, the class which Aristotle called the best safeguard against revolution, Sparta was obviously ripe for a change.

But during the fourth and third centuries there had grown up a belief that long ago Sparta had been a very different place; that Spartans had once owned no personal property but their weapons, and that their traditional lawgiver Lycurgus had divided the land equally among all Spartan citizens, who held it in equal lots; these lots had not exactly been the private property of their owners, but had been allotted to them by the State in order to enable them (since the lots were cultivated by Helots) to devote their time unhampered to the real business of the State, military training; just as a Spartan's body was not exactly his own, but in a sense be longed to the State, so did his land. The present state of things was regarded as a backsliding from this farmer ideal state. Of course this ideal state had never existed; there had always been rich and poor at Sparta, and there had never been, in historical times, an equal division of the land. But the idea was none the less powerful because it was really a product of philosophic speculations about communism. For the Stoics were teaching the equality of all men, and Zeno and Iambulus had constructed Utopias in which there were neither rich nor poor; and Iambulus is careful to explain that his people, having abolished classes, were ἀστασίαστοί, free from revolutionary troubles.

Now the poor in a Greek state had little chance of making a change constitutionally, and were badly off for weapons; they rather depended on a lead from some individual who was not one of themselves, and possessed some force, for instance mercenaries; this had been the case for example in the social revolution at Cassandreia, which had ended in a tyranny. By 244 the mixed Spartan constitution had become an oligarchy, and the ephors now ruled in the interest of the rich; hence the poor naturally looked for help to the kings. It is perfectly possible that Agis *was* partly a saint, as Phylarchus draws him — Plato's philosopher-king, inspired by Stoic teaching and the third century Utopias to create a new world of equality and brotherhood; and he may have had real sympathy for the poor. Probably he also had military ambition; for the military allotment, the κλῆρος, might be as potent a source of military strength to Sparta as it had been to the Hellenistic monarchies. But he was above all a Spartan patriot; he desired, without altering the political constitution, to restore what he believed to have been the golden age of Sparta by dividing the land equally into lots, so that all landless men should again receive allotments, and the common meals could be restored. But as he could not distribute mortgaged land, or usefully give allotments to poor men weighed down with debt, he had at the same time to envisage the cancellation of all debts, the State having no money to pay them; and so this very conservative reformer in fact adopted two of the main principles of the social revolution, division of and and cancellation of debt. (The Greeks of course hardly took our view of private debts; law-courts always favoured the debtor, and it is said that more than once debts had been discharged, even in mercantile Corinth, by the elementary process of killing the creditors.) As to the other two items in the full revolutionary programme, naturally Agis never considered freeing the Helots, who were a necessary part of the Lycurgan institutions — even the Stoics had never advocated abolition; and it is supposed that he did not mean to take personal property for the State. But he gave his own large fortune to the State, and hoped others would follow.

Though Agis thought he was going to restore an old state of things, he was really attempting quite a new one. But in a little country like Sparta, an equal division of the land, with a periodical redistribution, should have been perfectly feasible; one Greek community, the Liparaeans, did actually carry out such a redistribution every 20 years, treating the occupation of land as usufruct and not ownership. But as land at Sparta had in fact been private property for centuries, one can hardly blame the landowners for not suddenly becoming unselfish altruists merely because of a vague belief that once upon a time the State had had certain rights in the land. Whether Agis was justified in proposing to take their land for the good of the community is a matter on which I express no opinion; we are doing much the same thing, but more gradually, by means of the death duties. His actual proposal was to divide the land in the inner ring, about Sparta, into 4500 Spartan lots, and that in the outer ring into 15,000 lots for Perioeci; as there were nothing like 4500 Spartans, he proposed to fill up the number from Perioeci and selected metics in sympathy with Spartan institutions. One can see from the allusion to this in Teles' discourse *On Exile*, spoken at Megara two years after Agis' death, the great interest these proposals created.

The poor supported Agis heartily, with some of the young men, who caught the inspiration of youth. The only way to interpret what happened is to suppose that the landowners were divided into two parties. The wealthy, led by the other king Leonidas, were uncompromisingly hostile; many of them would be creditors. But those whose lands were mortgaged, led by Agis' uncle Agesilaus, the villain of the piece, thought they could make use of Agis to free their lands from debt. They first supported him; then, having captured the ephorate, they were able to prevent him carrying out both his proposals together, as he wished, and got debts abolished first, as they wished. They now had no further use for Agis; they sent him north with the army, and proceeded to undermine his position with the poor, who were disappointed at not getting the promised land; and when Agis returned, he found himself faced by the fact that he must use force or fail. He decided not to use force. Probably he could not trust the army; but it is quite possible that he deliberately preferred to die rather than kill his fellow-citizens. He took sanctuary, was captured by a trick, and murdered; a11d for a time Leonidas and the reaction triumphed.

Thirteen years later Agis' plans were taken up afresh by Leonidas' son Cleomenes, who had become king; he was a pupil of the Stoic Sphairos, and had married Agis' widow, and the two had converted him to Agis' views. He was a stronger and harder character than Agis, and not so single minded; and it weighed heavily with him that the reforms would greatly strengthen Sparta for war, for he was extremely ambitious. He saw clearly why Agis had failed; and though his aim was exactly the same, the restoration of the supposed Lycurgan institutions, one calls him a revolutionary and not a reformer because he saw that, to succeed, he must first overthrow the existing political constitution and overthrow it by force. All the Peloponnese except Elis, Messene and Sparta was now in the Achaean League, whose leading man was Aratus of Sicyon, a very clever, wealthy, and unprincipled statesman. Cleomenes began by picking a quarrel with the League and forcing Aratus to declare war; Phylarchus says he brought on the war simply to pave the way for his revolution, and the opposition writers, Aratus himself and Polybius, do not deny this. The war enabled Cleomenes to enlist mercenaries. When he was ready, he left the citizen troops in camp at a distance from Sparta, returned to Sparta with the mercenaries alone, turned out the ephors, killing four of them and ten of their supporters, exiled 80 others, and was sole master of Sparta with the loss of 14 lives. He then cancelled all debts, and divided the land very much as Agis had proposed; he also abolished the ephorate. In dividing the land, he set aside allotments for the 80 exiles, whom he meant to recall later. It shows that there was a touch of Alexander about Cleomenes; no one else had thought of recalling his political opponents.

Had Cleomenes stopped there; had he been content to make peace with Aratus and confine himself to the internal development of Sparta; one does not see what could have prevented his revolution being a permanent success. Sparta, which after Agis' death had been too weak to prevent even an Aetolian raid, had become at one stroke far too strong for any Greek state to attack; beside mercenaries, Cleomenes could put 14,000 to 15,000 Lacedaemonians into the field, as against the traditional 6000 of the fourth century. Unfortunately for Sparta, his ambition came into play; he wanted to be head of the Peloponnese, perhaps of Greece, and play Alexander in a new League of Corinth. He began by thoroughly defeating the Achaeans, and might have been elected head of the Achaean League had he not fallen ill just before the Achaean assembly met. Aratus tided over that danger; but what he could not tide over was that in several cities there had been a rising or revolution of the poorer classes which carried the city over to Cleomenes. The Achaean League was a most respectable institution, but it was based on the power of the well-to-do; and Aratus, who was terrified of social revolution, began to negotiate with Antigonus Doson of Macedonia for help to repress it. But as soon as this was known, Cleomenes swept the country; there were risings in many cities, including Argos and Corinth, and soon the Achaean League held nothing but Megalopolis and Sicyon, and even lost part of Achaea itself. It was a wave of revolutionary enthusiasm such as Greece had never seen; and Aratus, with his back to the wall, agreed to pay Antigonus' price, the cession of Corinth. Antigonus thereon formed a Greek League whose first object was to suppress the revolution; this follows from the fact that he gave out that he was not at war with Sparta but only with Cleomenes.

Probably we can now give one concrete instance of how Cleomenes' revolution affected other cities; that is the extraordinary little poem on wealth and poverty written by Cercidas. The writer is certainly the Cercidas who belonged to the governing class at Megalopolis and was a personal friend of Aratus; and Megalopolis was as hostile to Sparta as one city could be to another. And in face of this, Cercidas writes a poem questioning the justice of the gods in making some worthless men rich and better men poor, and then, turning to his own class in Megalopolis, declares that there is only one way for him and them; they must heal the sick and give to the poor while they have the chance, for, if not, their wealth may be taken away — the social revolution may be upon them. That a Greek politician of the upper classes should be advocating charity and philanthropy, even if only tentatively, even if partly perhaps through fear, is a most amazing phenomenon. Nothing came of it; for again Cleomenes' ambition drove Cercidas back into Aratus' arms.

And in fact Cleomenes' cause was lost, at the height of its success, before Antigonus intervened. That sweeping success had been largely due to the belief of the common people throughout the Peloponnese that he had come to give them the longed-for social revolution — land for everybody and no debts; what he had done at Sparta he would do elsewhere; there was going to be a new world. This was the last thing Cleomenes meant to do; he was a Spartan king, and had no idea of raising a whirlwind which might sweep himself away. It had already become clear, before Antigonus arrived, that Cleomenes was not going to introduce a general revolution; and the lower classes were ready to leave him and return to bearing the ills they knew of. Consequently, when Aratus man aged to slip a few troops into Argos behind Cleomenes' back — he was at the Isthmus — Argos changed sides; and Cleomenes, with his communications threatened, had to quit the Isthmus and retreat to cover Sparta, while city after city fell away. He had suffered the usual fate of the moderate revolutionary, and antagonized both parties, both the well-to-do and the poor, the one because he went too far,the other because he did not go far enough. The rest is only fighting; he had his revenge on Megalopolis, but was defeated by Antigonus at Sellasia and fled to Egypt, perhaps the only king of Sparta who ever survived a great defeat; and I know nothing in later Greek literature sadder than the speech in which Plutarch makes him justify his choice between his duty to die and his duty to live for Sparta and the revolution.

Antigonus restored the old *régime* at Sparta, and many of Cleoinenes' new citizens lost their land again. But his party was not destroyed; and the city led an unsettled existence for 14 years, with an increasing number of exiles, till in 207 it was badly defeated by the Achaeans. Thereon the real revolution, which must long have been smouldering, broke out under the lead of a man called Nabis. All we know about Nabis comes from his hitter enemies. He may have been as cruel as Polybius says he was — though Polybius himself could advocate torture with anybody — and his mercenaries may have been the scum of the earth; but one must look fairly at what he did. He carried out all the four points of the social revolution; he not only abolished debts and redistributed the land, but he took all the money he could get from the well-to-do, many of whom he exiled, I and freed slaves; part of his army was composed of liberated Helots. When Argos was given to him by Philip V, he apparently carried out the social revolution there in much the same way. But he professed that the money which he exacted from the rich was taken "for the common expenses of the State," and it seems possible that the State now paid for the common meals, as was done in Crete; and Polybius in a later book accidentally shows that he left the wives and daughters of the exiles in undisturbed possession of a certain amount of land. Certainly in getting rid of the class state, as he claimed to have done, and substituting one in which all were equal, he for the last time restored Sparta's strength in an extraordinary manner. In spite of her terrible losses by war and exile, he raised 10,000 citizen troops, partly, liberated Helots, and with mercenaries and 2000 Argives — evidently he could trust the lower classes at Argos — he had in Sparta 18,000 men when Rome declared war on him; and when Flamininus, the conqueror of Macedonia, attacked Sparta with 50,000 men, they beat him off. One can see that they must have fought for *some* sort of an idea, anyhow. Certainly Nabis lost his nerve and accepted Flamininus' terms next day; but though he lost Argos and the coast, Flamininus made no attempt to alter anything in Sparta itself, or restore the exiles. When Nabis was assassinated by the Aetolians, the people rose and avenged him ; and when the chaos after his death ended in Philopoemen joining Sparta to the Achaean League, recalling the exiles, and brutally abolishing the peculiar Spartan training and institutions, 3000 of Nabis' new citizens refused to go to Achaea with Philopoemen and preferred to take the consequences; Philopoemen sold them as slaves. So the revolution at Sparta finally ended as Polybius says that revolutions in Greece always did end, in the ruin of the community that made them. But that it did so end was due entirely to Cleomenes' ambition and to foreign enemies.